healthy hearty meals

daniel green
healthy hearty meals

Series Designer: Bernard Go Kwang Meng

Copyright © 2013 Marshall Cavendish International (Asia) Private Limited

Published by Marshall Cavendish Cuisine
An imprint of Marshall Cavendish International

All rights reserved

No part of this publication may be reproduced, stored in a retrieval system or transmitted, in any form or by any means, electronic, mechanical, photocopying, recording or otherwise, without the prior permission of the copyright owner. Request for permission should be addressed to the Publisher, Marshall Cavendish International (Asia) Private Limited, 1 New Industrial Road, Singapore 536196. Tel: (65) 6213 9300   Fax: (65) 6285 4871
E-mail: genref@sg.marshallcavendish.com   Online bookstore: http://www.marshallcavendish.com

The Intellectual Property of Daniel Green, its brand expression "The Model Cook" and all related indicia presented herein are owned and exclusively managed by Astra Worldwide Limited, Hong Kong.
For all enquiries, please contact vivien.lee@astraonair.com

Limits of Liability/Disclaimer of Warranty: The Author and Publisher of this book have used their best efforts in preparing this book. The Publisher makes no representation or warranties with respect to the contents of this book and is not responsible for the outcome of any recipe in this book. While the Publisher has reviewed each recipe carefully, the reader may not always achieve the results desired due to variations in ingredients, cooking temperatures and individual cooking abilities. The Publisher shall in no event be liable for any loss of profit or any other commercial damage, including but not limited to special, incidental, consequential, or other damages.

Other Marshall Cavendish Offices:
Marshall Cavendish Corporation. 99 White Plains Road, Tarrytown NY 10591-9001, USA • Marshall Cavendish International (Thailand) Co Ltd. 253 Asoke, 12th Flr, Sukhumvit 21 Road, Klongtoey Nua, Wattana, Bangkok 10110, Thailand • Marshall Cavendish (Malaysia) Sdn Bhd, Times Subang, Lot 46, Subang Hi-Tech Industrial Park, Batu Tiga, 40000 Shah Alam, Selangor Darul Ehsan, Malaysia

Marshall Cavendish is a trademark of Times Publishing Limited

National Library Board, Singapore Cataloguing-in-Publication Data

Green, Daniel, 1970-.
Healthy hearty meals / Daniel Green. – Singapore : Marshall Cavendish Cuisine, c2013.
p. cm.
ISBN : 978-981-4408-06-6 (pbk.)

1. Cooking. 2. Cookbooks. 3. Low-fat diet -- Recipes. I. Title

TX7145
641.56384 -- dc23   OCN811576561

Printed in Singapore by Saik Wah Print Media Pte Ltd

vegetable stock 9
chicken stock 9
udon noodles in broth 10
noodle soup 13
vietnamese hot and sour soup 14
low-fat mushroom soup 17
parsnip and sweet potato soup 18
potato salad 21
italian seafood salad 22
vietnamese noodle salad 25
slow-cooked beef stew 26
mum's pan-fried chicken 29

contents

roasted butternut squash 30
prawns with green beans 33
minced chicken dumplings 34
steamed pot stickers 37
vietnamese rolls 38
east meets west crab cakes 40
sea bass wrapped in seaweed 43
miso salmon 44
steamed sea bass 47
fish burger 48
roast chicken with sun-dried tomato risotto 50
masala chicken 52
chicken napoli 55

lemon chicken 56
saffron chicken 59
roast lamb 60
beef yakitori 63
roasted vegetables 64
spicy chilli calamari 67
wasabi crust tuna 68
truffle risotto 71
egg fried rice 72
gnocchi in tomato sauce 75
tomato and crab spaghetti 76
egg noodles with chicken and vegetables 79
weights and measures 80

vegetable stock

Makes about 625 ml (20 fl oz / 2^1/$_2$ cups)

Making your own stock need not be a chore. This vegetable stock is easy to make and you'll see for yourself the difference in the taste alone.

INGREDIENTS

Carrots	2, chopped
Onions	2, peeled and quartered
Celery	2 sticks, chopped
Fennel bulb	^{1}/$_2$, chopped
Stalk from a head of broccoli	1, chopped
Large tomatoes	4
Button mushrooms	8, halved
Black peppercorns	6
Bay leaf	1
Tomato paste	4 Tbsp
Parsley	3 stalks
Water	1 litre (32 fl oz / 4 cups)

METHOD

- Place all ingredients in a large pot and simmer for about 50 minutes.
- Strain the stock before use.

chicken stock

Makes about 625 ml (20 fl oz / 2^1/$_2$ cups)

The key to a good low-fat chicken stock is to refrigerate it, then skim off the fat from the surface. Home-made stocks can be stored in the refrigerator for 2–3 days and up to a month in the freezer.

INGREDIENTS

Chicken	1, medium, cut into 8 pieces
Button mushrooms	6, halved
Salt	^{1}/$_2$ tsp
Black peppercorns	1 tsp
Carrots	2, chopped
Onions	2 peeled and quartered
Celery	2 sticks, chopped
Garlic	3 cloves
Large tomatoes	4
Parsley	3 stalks
Water	1 litre (32 fl oz / 4 cups)

METHOD

- Place all ingredients in a large pot and simmer for about 50 minutes.
- Strain the stock before use.

udon noodles in broth Serves 4

Udon noodles are my latest craving. They are healthy and so filling and yet I cannot seem to get enough.

INGREDIENTS

Udon noodles	700 g (1 1/2 lb)
Vegetable stock (page 9)	500 ml (16 fl oz / 2 cups)
Soft bean curd	250 g (9 oz), cubed
Light soy sauce	1 Tbsp
Spring onions (scallions)	4, chopped

METHOD

- Boil the noodles in water for a few minutes and drain.
- Heat the stock and add the noodles, bean curd, soy sauce and spring onions.
- Cook for 2–3 minutes and serve.

noodle soup Serves 4

There are times when I have arrived in Hong Kong jet-lagged and in need of food. I usually call for room service and order a bowl of wonton noodle soup. This recipe reminds me of the comfort I can get from a bowl of warm noodle soup. It hits the spot every time.

INGREDIENTS

Chicken stock (page 9)	150 ml (5 fl oz)
Egg noodles	450 g (1 lb)
Mushrooms	12, sliced
Sesame oil	1 Tbsp
Light soy sauce	1 Tbsp
Garlic	1 clove, peeled and crushed
Tiger prawns	6, peeled, leaving tails intact

METHOD

- In a small pot, heat the chicken stock until simmering.
- Add all the remaining ingredients and cook for 4–5 minutes, until the prawns turn pink and are cooked. Remove from the heat and serve.

vietnamese hot and sour soup Serves 8

The Chinese have their own version of hot and sour soup, but the Vietnamese recipe is more flavourful, with the use of fresh herbs and chillies.

INGREDIENTS

Cooking oil	2 Tbsp
Onion	1, peeled and thinly sliced
Garlic	2 cloves, peeled and crushed
Red chillies	1–2, seeded and minced
Vegetable stock (page 9)	1.75 litres (56 fl oz / 7 cups)
Canned straw mushrooms	1 small can, drained
Tomatoes	1 cup, chopped
Firm bean curd	200 g (7 oz), cut into cubes
Eggs	2, beaten
Mung bean sprouts	a handful
Coriander leaves (cilantro)	a handful, chopped
Freshly squeezed lime juice	2 Tbsp
Light soy sauce	2 Tbsp

METHOD

- Heat oil in a large pan and fry the onion until soft. Add garlic and chillies and sauté for another minute.

- Stir in the stock, mushrooms and tomatoes and bring to the boil. Lower heat and simmer for 5 minutes.

- Add the bean curd, then drizzle in the egg, stirring, so it sets as thin strips.

- Season with soy sauce and lime juice. Add the bean sprouts and coriander and remove from heat.

- Serve hot with rice.

low-fat mushroom soup Serves 4–6

When I first started cooking, I created an amazing cappuccino of mushroom sauce. I made it for my in-laws, Jennifer and Tony, and my mum and dad. I never told them how much fat was in it and that was why I never ate it myself. But since then, I have come up with a better low fat version. And here it is.

INGREDIENTS

Potatoes	450 g (1 lb), peeled, cut into 1.3-cm ($1/2$-in) cubes
Extra virgin olive oil	3 Tbsp
Large onion	1, peeled and chopped
Garlic	1 clove, peeled and crushed
Button mushrooms	450 g (1 lb) with stems, coarsely chopped
Dry sherry	4 Tbsp
Chicken stock (page 9)	250 ml (8 fl oz / 1 cup)
Low-fat milk	375 ml (12 fl oz / $1^{1}/_{2}$ cups)

METHOD

- Heat a pot of water and boil the potatoes for 25 minutes. Drain and set aside.

- In a large non-stick pan, add the extra virgin olive oil over medium-high heat. Add the onion and garlic, and cook for 2 minutes.

- Add the mushrooms and cook for 3–4 minutes. Add the sherry and cook for a minute, then add the stock and simmer for 10 minutes.

- In a blender, place the boiled potatoes, milk and everything from the pan and process until smooth.

- Reheat if desired and serve immediately.

parsnip and sweet potato soup Serves 6

With a taste of the Mediterranean, this soup is rich and creamy even without the addition of cream. It's filling and delightfully easy to do. Give it a try!

INGREDIENTS

Olive oil	1 Tbsp
Onion	1, peeled and cut into quarters
Sweet potato	1, large, peeled and cut into chunks
Parsnips	6, peeled and cut into chunks
Vegetable stock (page 9)	1 litre (32 fl oz / 4 cups)
Skimmed milk	625 ml (20 fl oz / $2^{1}/_{2}$ cups)
Chives	

CROUTONS

White bread	4 slices
Olive oil	

METHOD

- Preheat the oven to 90°C (370°F).

- Prepare the croutons. Cut the bread into small cubes and place in a roasting pan. Drizzle with olive oil and mix well. Bake for 10 minutes.

- Heat oil in a large saucepan. Add the onion but do not allow it to brown. Cook for about 1 minute, then add sweet potato and parsnips. Cook for 3 minutes, then add the stock and stir well. When the stock comes to the boil, lower heat and add the milk. Leave to simmer for 25 minutes.

- When ready, place a handheld blender in the saucepan and blend thoroughly. Alternatively, pour the contents of the saucepan into a blender and process.

- Reheat the soup if desired. Serve soup in bowls, topped with a few croutons and sprinkled with chives.

potato salad Serves 4

I developed this recipe for my buddy Layne when he asked for a low-fat potato salad.

INGREDIENTS
Baby potatoes	900 g (2 lb), sliced in half
Extra virgin olive oil	4 Tbsp
Dijon mustard	2 Tbsp
Chives	a handful, finely chopped

METHOD
- Boil a pot of water and cook the potatoes for 20–25 minutes. Remove and drain.
- Whisk the extra virgin olive oil and Dijon mustard until it resembles mayonnaise. Add the chives.
- Toss the potatoes with the sauce and serve.

italian seafood salad Serves 2–4

It does not get better than this classic, naturally healthy and flavourful salad dish. I could eat this all day long. It was at a train station in Milan where I first had this outrageous seafood salad from a little café. It is true that the Italians are passionate about food!

INGREDIENTS

Sea scallops	225 g (8 oz)
Medium prawns	110 g (4 oz)
Fresh mussels	225 g (4 oz)
Squid rings	110 g (4 oz)
Pitted kalamata olives	$1/2$ cup
Lemon juice	2 Tbsp
Extra virgin olive oil	85 ml ($2^1/2$ fl oz / $1/3$ cup)
Garlic	1 large clove, peeled and minced
Chopped fresh parsley	1 Tbsp
Chopped fresh chives	1 Tbsp
Red chilli flakes	$1/4$ tsp
Mixed salad greens	6 cups
Lemon	1, sliced
Red onion	1, medium, peeled and thinly sliced
Sea salt	to taste
Freshly ground black pepper	to taste

METHOD

- Bring a large pot of water to boil and place the scallops, prawns, mussels and squid in the boiling water to cook for 2 minutes. Drain. Peel the prawns, and shell the scallops and mussels.

- Place cooked seafood and olives in a large bowl, and toss with lemon juice, extra virgin olive oil, garlic, parsley, chives and red chilli flakes. Chill for 1 hour.

- Divide salad greens among individual serving plates or salad bowls. Spoon seafood over salad greens and garnish with slices of lemon and red onion. Season with salt and freshly ground black pepper.

vietnamese noodle salad serves 4–6

Vietnamese cuisine is rich in its use of fresh herbs which gives its dishes a clean and refreshing flavour. This noodle salad testifies to that. Peanuts are high in fat, so omit them if preferred.

INGREDIENTS

Small prawns (shrimps)	450 g (1 lb)
Dried rice noodles	125 g (4 1/2 oz), soaked in water to soften
Crabmeat	300 g (11 oz) (canned is fine)
Cucumbers	300 g (11 oz), sliced
Radish	150 g (5 1/3 oz), sliced
Unsalted peanuts (optional)	75 g (2 1/2 oz), chopped
Coriander leaves (cilantro)	a handful, chopped
Chopped mint leaves	a handful

DRESSING

Sugar	2 Tbsp
Vietnamese fish sauce	3 Tbsp
Lemon juice	from 1 lemon
Small red chillies	1–2, seeds removed and finely sliced
Garlic	2 cloves, peeled and crushed
Finely grated ginger	2 tsp

METHOD

- Combine all the ingredients for the dressing in a bowl and mix well. Set aside.
- Bring a pot of water to the boil and cook prawns. Drain. When cool enough to handle, peel prawns and set aside.
- Drain the noodles and place into a large salad bowl. Add the prawns, other remaining ingredients and dressing. Toss well and serve.

slow-cooked beef stew Serves 6

I recommend doubling the quantities on this as it gets better and better with keeping and reheating. I will probably add this to my creations for the KLM inflight menu as not many dishes can stand up to being reheated like this one!

INGREDIENTS

Extra virgin olive oil	1 Tbsp
Lean beef	1.4 kg (3 lb), cut into cubes
Onion	1, peeled and diced
Red wine	50 ml (1 $^2/_3$ fl oz)
Plain (all-purpose) flour	1 tsp
Baby carrots	12
Baby potatoes	12, halved
Brussel sprouts	12
Garlic	3 cloves, peeled and crushed
Beef stock	50 ml (1 $^2/_3$ fl oz), made using stock cubes and water, according to instructions on packet

METHOD

- Heat a large stockpot that has a cover and retains heat well. Add the extra virgin olive oil and fry the beef cubes for 3–4 minutes until browned on all sides.

- Add the onion and fry for a few minutes. Add the red wine and lower heat to a simmer. Whisk the flour into the stock, then add it and everything else to the pot. Cover and simmer over very low heat for 40 minutes until beef is very tender.

- Dish out and serve hot.

mum's pan-fried chicken Serves 4

My mum used to cook dinner for us every day, always preparing it with fresh ingredients and lots of love. I asked her for this recipe when I started to develop a love for cooking. This was a dish I grew up eating. Thanks to the best mum in the world!

INGREDIENTS

Plain (all-purpose) flour	1 Tbsp
Salt	to taste
Ground pepper	to taste
Skinless, boneless chicken fillets	4, cut into bite-size pieces
Extra virgin olive oil	1 Tbsp
Red capsicum (bell pepper)	1, diced
Onion	$1/2$, peeled and chopped
Garlic	1 clove, peeled and crushed
Cherry tomatoes	6, sliced
Carrots	2, peeled and cut into small cubes
Mushrooms	6, sliced
Canned or frozen peas	1 cup
Water	125 ml (4 fl oz / $1/2$ cup)

METHOD

- Put the flour in a plastic bag and add salt, pepper and chicken shaking it around until chicken is well-coated.

- Heat extra virgin olive oil in a wok and add the chicken. Stir-fry until almost cooked. Remove the chicken to a plate.

- Reheat the wok and add the capsicum, onion, garlic, tomatoes, carrots, mushrooms, peas and stir-fry for a few minutes to mix well. Add water and allow to boil.

- Return chicken to the wok and stir-fry until chicken is cooked through. Season with salt and pepper.

- Dish out and serve immediately.

roasted butternut squash Serves 4

Feel like you want to binge on carbs? Then try this dish which will satisfy your craving, but yet is low on carbs and fat! My mum taught me this one, and I added the garlic.

INGREDIENTS

Butternut squash	2
Extra virgin olive oil	2–3 Tbsp
Garlic	1 bulb, cut in half horizontally
Rock salt	2 tsp

METHOD

- Preheat the oven to 230°C (450°F).
- Peel the butternut squash and slice in half. Take out the seeds and discard. Place the butternut squash in a roasting pan. Drizzle over with extra virgin olive oil.
- Place the bulb of garlic on a sheet of aluminium foil. Drizzle the two halves with 1 Tbsp extra virgin olive oil, place the halves together and wrap with foil. Place in the roasting pan with the butternut squash.
- Roast for 40–50 minutes. Unwrap the bulb of garlic, being careful not to scorch your fingers. Squeeze out the meat from each clove of garlic which has been baked to a soft consistency. Sprinkle rock salt on garlic and butternut squash.
- Serve immediately.

prawns with green beans Serves 4

This is a nice mix of protein and some carbs. Try this with canned tuna too!

INGREDIENTS

Prawns (shrimps)	450 g (1 lb), peeled and deveined
Green beans	300 g (11 oz), ends trimmed
Red onion	1/4, peeled and finely sliced

DRESSING

Capers	1 Tbsp, chopped
Extra virgin olive oil	2 Tbsp
Lemon juice	from 1/2 lemon
Dijon mustard	1 tsp
Fresh basil leaves	a handful, chopped

METHOD

- Boil a pot of water and poach prawns in it for 3–5 minutes or until prawns turn pink. Remove prawns, drain and set aside.

- Boil another pot of water and add the green beans. Cook for 6 minutes. Drain and place in a mixing bowl. Add the prawns and onion.

- Mix the dressing ingredients in another bowl, then add to the bean and prawn mixture. Toss well and serve.

minced chicken dumplings serves 6–8

I love dim sum and these minced chicken dumplings are one of my favourites. They are easy to do and you can use anything for the filling from pork to prawns.

INGREDIENTS

Lean minced chicken	450 g (1 lb)
Egg	1
Light soy sauce	1 Tbsp
Garlic	2 cloves, peeled
Ginger	2.5-cm (1-in) knob, peeled
Sesame oil	1 Tbsp
Spring onion (scallion)	1, finely chopped

DUMPLING SKIN

Wheat starch (*tang meen fun*)	160 g (5^2/$_3$ oz)
Tapioca (cassava) flour	160 g (5^2/$_3$ oz)
Cooking oil	4 Tbsp
Salt	^{1}/$_2$ tsp
Hot water	180–200 ml (6–7 fl oz)

METHOD

- Process all the ingredients for the filling, except spring onion, into a paste, then mix in chopped spring onion. Set aside.

- Prepare dumpling skin. Put flours, oil and salt in the mixing bowl of an electric mixer fitted with a dough hook. Add hot water gradually while beating on low speed until a soft, smooth dough is achieved.

- Roll dough out into a long cylindrical shape, then cut into small rounds. Roll each round out thinly into a disc about 7.5-cm (3-in) in diameter.

- Place a disc of dough in the palm of your hand. Place 2 tsp filling in the centre, then pleat the edges, pressing to seal dumpling. Repeat until ingredients are used up.

- Brush the base of a steaming basket with oil and place dumplings in. Cook in batches if the steamer basket is small. Steam for 8–10 minutes.

- Serve hot with some light soy sauce or chilli sauce on the side.

steamed pot stickers serves 6–8

Unlike the pot stickers served in restaurants, these are steamed, not pan-fried in oil, so they are much healthier, but just as tasty!

INGREDIENTS

Pot sticker wrappers	18–24, available from supermarkets
Egg	1, beaten

FILLING

Lean minced chicken	225 g (8 oz)
Prawns (shrimps)	225 g (8 oz), peeled
Spring onions (scallions)	4, chopped
Bacon	2 rashers
White sesame seeds	1 Tbsp
Chopped coriander leaves (cilantro)	2 Tbsp
Light soy sauce	1 Tbsp
Egg white	1

METHOD

- Process all the ingredients for the filling until mixed but still chunky.
- Place a pot sticker wrapper in the palm of your hand. Top with a teaspoonful of filling, then brush edges with some egg and fold over in half. Crimp edges to seal. Continue until ingredients are used up.
- Brush the base of a steaming basket with oil and place pot stickers in. Cover and steam for about 20 minutes.
- Serve hot with some light soy sauce or chilli sauce on the side.

vietnamese rolls Serves 4

This dish is popular all over the world. It is usually the first dish that comes to mind when people think of Vietnamese food. The best Vietnamese rolls I had was in Bangkok, at a restaurant where my friends, Yoon and Clive took me to. It was so incredible, I just had to replicate it here.

INGREDIENTS

Rice vermicelli	50 g (1^{2}/$_{3}$ oz), soaked in warm water to soften
Prawns (shrimps)	12
Mung bean sprouts	150 g (5^{1}/$_{3}$ oz)
Large carrot	1, peeled and shredded
Sugar	1 tsp
Fish sauce	1 Tbsp
Vietnamese rice paper	8 sheets
Lettuce leaves	8 (any kind of lettuce will do)
Small cucumber	1, cut into strips
Mint leaves	a handful

DIPPING SAUCE

Red chillies	5, finely chopped
Water	150 ml (5 fl oz)
White wine vinegar	150 ml (5 fl oz)

METHOD

- Start by preparing the dipping sauce. Place all the ingredients in a small pan and simmer over medium heat for about 10 minutes or until the mixture is slightly thickened like a sauce. Set aside in a bowl.
- Bring a pot of water to the boil and cook vermicelli for 2–3 minutes. Remove with a strainer and drain well. Set aside.
- Bring a fresh pot of water to the boil and add prawns. When prawns turn pink and are cooked, remove and drain. Peel when cool.
- Mix vermicelli with shredded carrot, sugar and fish sauce.

- Dip a rice sheet in warm water, then drain and lay it on a flat work surface. Top with a lettuce leaf followed by a spoonful of carrot and noodle mix, a few prawns, cucumber, bean sprouts and a few mint leaves. Roll up, cut in half and arrange on a serving plate. Repeat until ingredients are used up.
- Serve Vietnamese rolls with dipping sauce on the side.

east meets west crab cakes Serves 4

Crab cakes are typically deep-fried, so I came up with this version which allows me to enjoy all the taste without the fat. These appetisers are easy to make and will always be a welcome treat! Lump crab meat, which is meat from the body chamber of the crab, works well in this recipe.

INGREDIENTS

Day-old white bread	4 slices
Red bird's eye chilli	1
Garlic	1/2 clove, peeled
Small onion	1/2, peeled
Ground coriander	1 Tbsp
Eggs	4
Egg whites	2
Fresh or premium canned crab meat	450 g (1 lb)
Sesame oil	1 Tbsp
Lime or lemon juice	from 1 lime or lemon
Light soy sauce	1 Tbsp
Olive oil	3–4 Tbsp

METHOD

- Process bread into fine crumbs. Divide into 2 equal portions. Set aside.

- Put chilli, garlic, onion, coriander, 2 eggs and egg whites to the blender and process until smooth. Transfer mixture to a large bowl and add a portion of breadcrumbs, crab meat, sesame oil, lime or lemon juice and soy sauce. (Placing all the ingredients into the blender together will make the mixture too fine. Mixing some of the ingredients by hand helps retain the texture and flavour.)

- Using your hands, form the mixture into small patties.

- Whisk remaining eggs and place in a shallow bowl. Place remaining portion of breadcrumbs into another shallow bowl.

- Heat 1–2 Tbsp oil in a large pan over high heat. Dip one patty at a time into whisked eggs, then coat with breadcrumbs. Place into the pan and cook for 2 minutes on each side. Turn the heat down if the patties brown too quickly. Drain well and serve with salad greens.

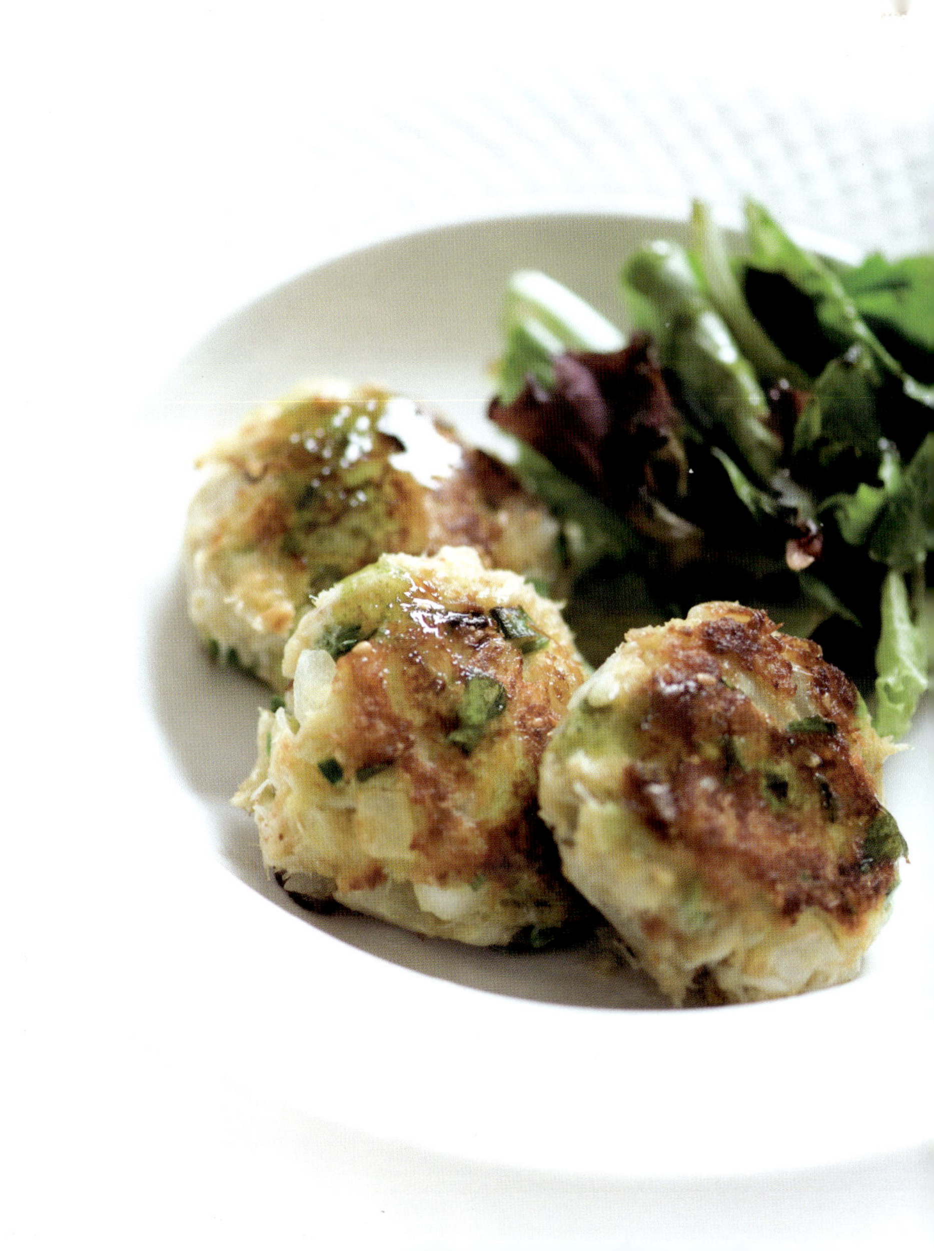

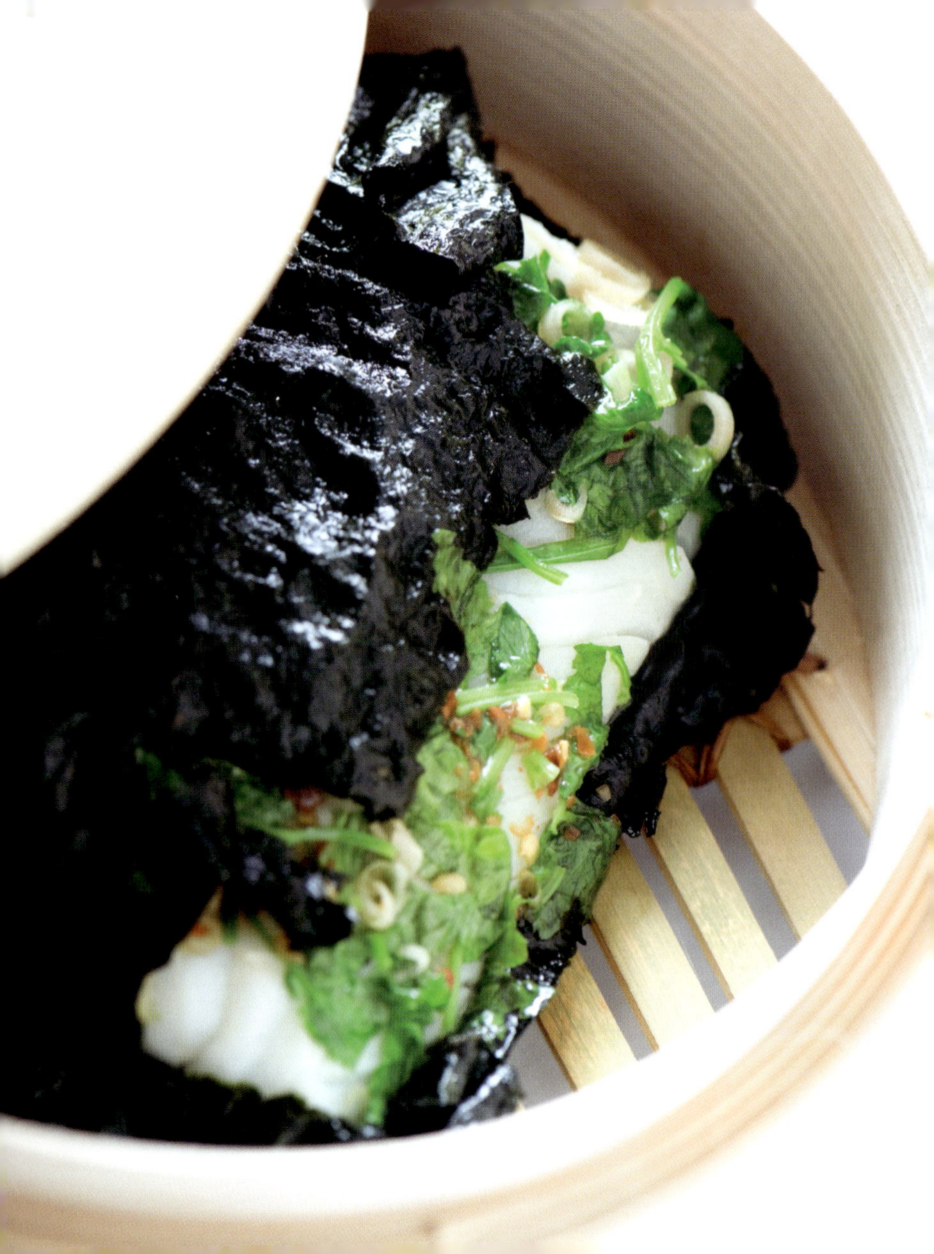

sea bass wrapped in seaweed Serves 4

I created this dish as I love how seaweed is used in Japanese cooking as a wrap for rice, but don't always want to fill myself up with rice. This dish looks rather pretty when it is cut through the middle.

INGREDIENTS

Ginger	2.5-cm (1-in) knob, peeled and grated
Lime juice	from 1 lime
Garlic	1 clove, peeled and crushed
Sesame oil	1 tsp
Light soy sauce	1 Tbsp
Small red chilli	1, finely chopped
Coriander leaves (cilantro)	a handful, chopped
Sea bass fillets	4, each 110–140 g (4–5 oz)
Seaweed (nori)	8 sheets

METHOD

- Combine ginger, lime juice, garlic, sesame oil, soy sauce, chilli and coriander leaves in a bowl. Set aside.

- Pat fish fillets dry, then place a fillet on a sheet of seaweed. Spread a quarter of the seasoning mix over fish. Bring sides of seaweed up over fish, then cover with another sheet of seaweed. Dampen the seaweed if necessary to cover the fish. Repeat for all the fillets.

- Place fish in separate steaming baskets and steam for 15–18 minutes until the fish is cooked through. The flesh should flake easily when pierced with a fork.

- Garnish as desired and serve hot.

miso salmon Serves 2

As part of my work with KLM Royal Dutch Airlines, I create dishes that are served on their flights. This modern, tasty Japanese dish is one I designed for their transatlantic routes into Amsterdam.

INGREDIENTS

Salmon	2 fillets, each 110–140 g (4–5 oz)

MARINADE

Grated ginger	1 Tbsp
Garlic	1 clove, peeled and crushed
Honey	2–3 Tbsp
Mirin	3 Tbsp
Miso paste	2 Tbsp
Lemon juice	from 1 large lemon

METHOD

- Mix ingredients for the marinade together in a bowl.
- Brush salmon with the marinade.
- Preheat the oven to 200°C (400°F).
- Place salmon under the grill for 3–4 minutes for a light crust to form, then transfer it to the oven to bake for 7–8 minutes, basting it once or twice.
- In the meantime, bring remaining marinade to the boil. for serving as a sauce.
- Serve salmon hot with rice and extra sauce on the side.

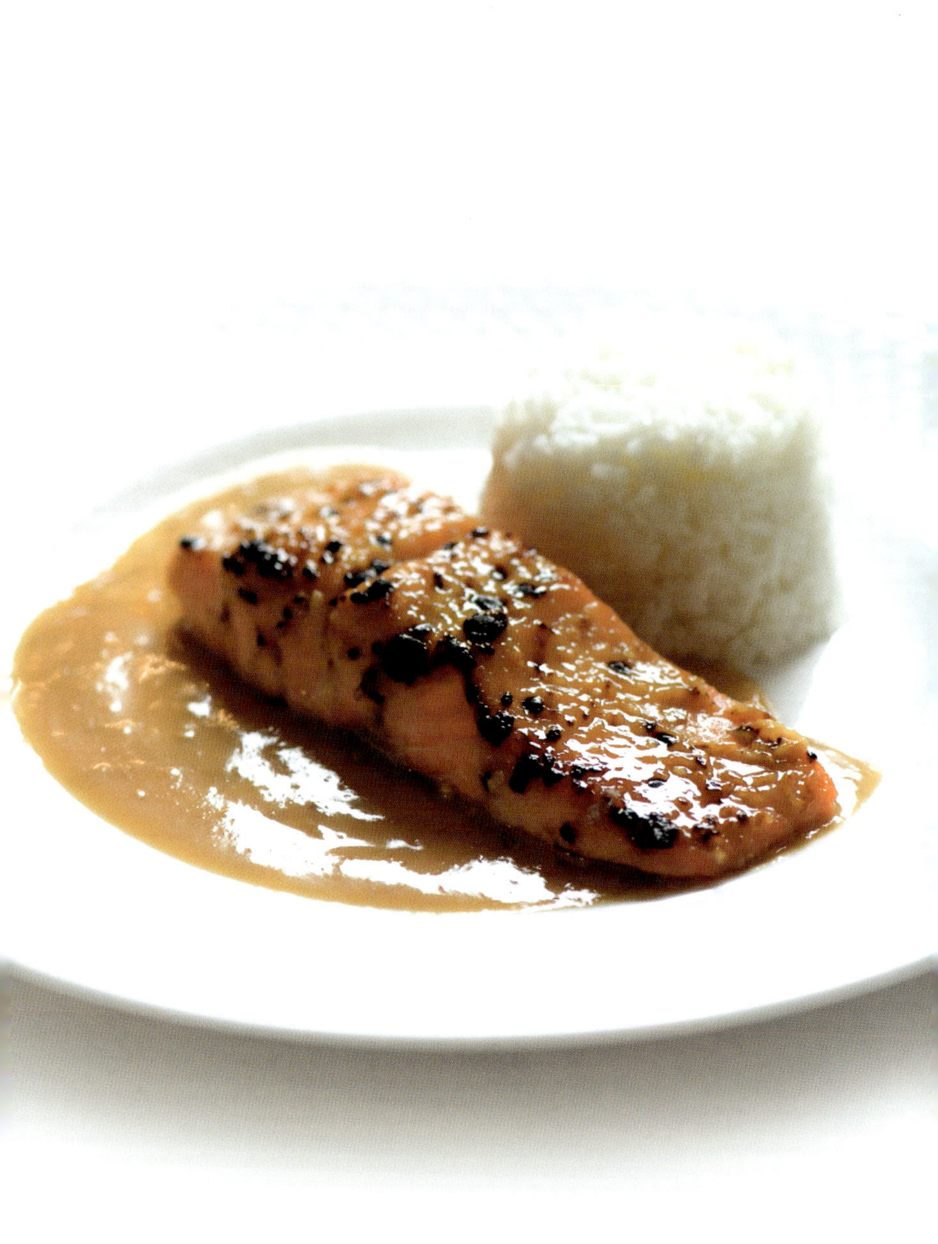

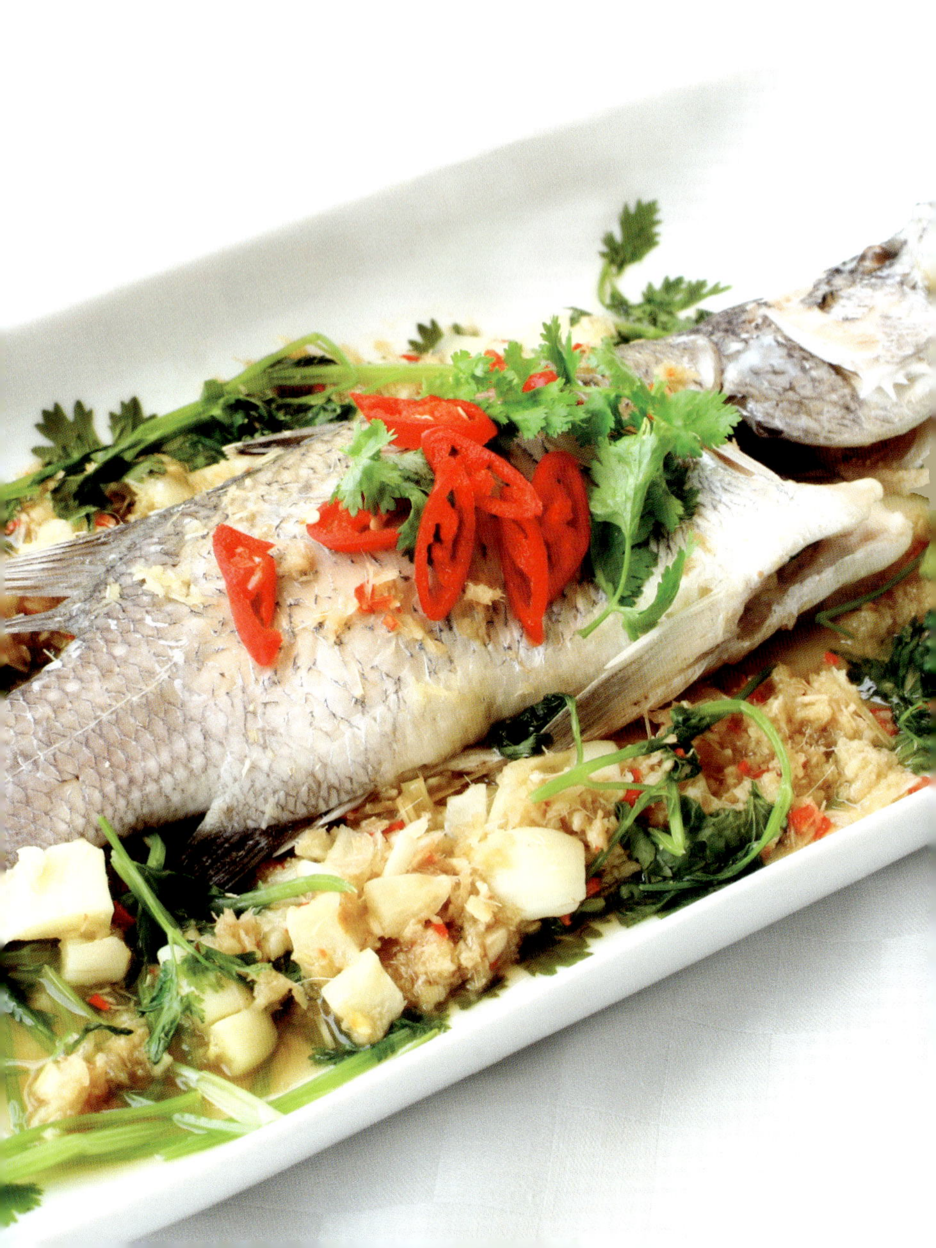

steamed sea bass Serves 4

Sea bass is farmed in Thailand. The fish has a delicate flavour and tastes wonderful steamed.

INGREDIENTS

Sea bass	1, about 500 g (1 lb 1 1/2 oz), gutted and cleaned
Coriander leaves (cilantro)	200 g (7 oz)

SAUCE

Thai fish sauce	1 Tbsp
Garlic	1 clove, peeled and crushed
Red chilli	1, finely chopped
Grated ginger	1 Tbsp
Lemon grass	3 stalks, tough outer leaves removed and finely chopped

METHOD

- Combine all the ingredients for the sauce in a bowl and set aside.

- Make a few cuts on both sides of fish.

- Arrange coriander on a steaming tray, then place fish on top. Pour sauce over and steam for 12 minutes, or until fish is cooked. The flesh should flake easily when pierced with a fork.

- Garnish as desired and serve immediately with rice.

fish burger <small>Serves 4</small>

The fish patty in a fish burger need not be deep-fried. I had the best grilled fish burger in the Florida Keys. The reason it was so delicious was the freshness of the mahi-mahi fish used. Try it with this recipe, if it's available to you. Here, the fish is lightly pan-fried.

INGREDIENTS

Ciabatta loaf	1
Eggs	2
Bread	2 slices
Olive oil	as needed
Mahi-mahi, halibut, seabass or snowfish	4 fillets
Non-fat sour cream or non-fat yoghurt	8 Tbsp
Lime juice and zest	from 1 lime
Chopped tarragon	1 Tbsp
Rocket (arugula) leaves	a handful

METHOD

- Cut ciabatta into 4 equal pieces, then slice each piece horizontally across in half. Toast and set aside.
- Beat eggs in a bowl.
- Place sliced bread into a blender and process into crumbs. Pour crumbs into a clean bowl.
- Heat a little oil in a frying pan over medium heat.
- Dip each fish fillet into beaten egg, then into breadcrumbs and fry for about 4 minutes on each side, or until cooked, depending on the thickness of the fish.
- Meanwhile, make tartar sauce. Combine sour cream or yoghurt with lime zest and juice and tarragon.
- Sandwich fish with the toasted ciabatta, topped with a spoonful of tartar sauce and some rocket leaves. Garnish as desired and serve immediately.

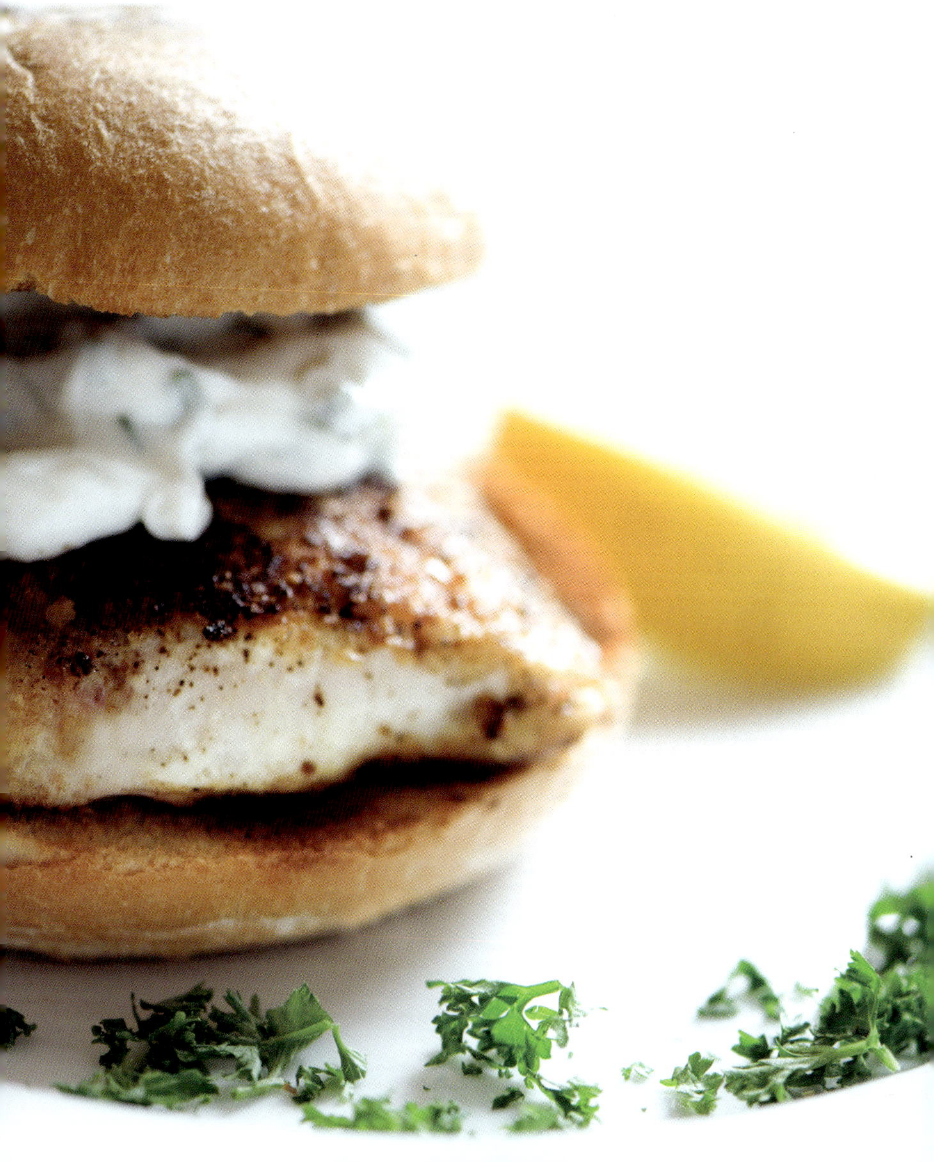

roast chicken with sun-dried tomato risotto

Serves 4–6

Roast chicken can sometimes be bland, but not with this recipe! Paired with a smooth risotto, this recipe is Italian food at its best!

INGREDIENTS

Chicken	1 whole, large (corn-fed if available)
Chicken or vegetable stock cubes	4, crushed
Garlic	4–6 cloves, with skin, cut into halves
Lemons	2, cut into quarters
Rosemary	2 sprigs

RISOTTO

Chicken stock (page 9)	1 litre (32 fl oz / 4 cups)
Olive oil	3 Tbsp
Large onion	1, peeled and finely chopped
Garlic	2 cloves, crushed
White wine (optional)	250 ml (8 fl oz / 1 cup)
Risotto rice	300 g (11 oz)
Tomato paste	1 Tbsp
Sun-dried tomatoes	12, finely chopped

METHOD

- Rinse chicken through the cavity to clean. Drain well.

- Add a few pieces of stock cube into cavity of chicken, followed with a few halves of garlic, then a quarter of lemon, squeezing it as you push it in. Repeat this process until all the ingredients are stuffed into the chicken. Lastly, slide in rosemary.

- Place chicken in a roasting pan and roast in an oven preheated to 220°C (440°F) for 1 hour or until chicken is done.

- While chicken is roasting, prepare risotto. Bring stock to the boil.

- Heat oil in a large pan and add onion. Cook for 2–3 minutes, then add garlic and sauté for a minute. Add risotto rice and stir so rice is well-coated with oil.

- Add wine and cook for a minute. Add boiling chicken stock one ladle at a time, stirring constantly for 20 minutes until rice is al dente. About 5 minutes before rice is ready, add tomato paste and chopped sun-dried tomatoes.

- To serve, place a small round cutter on a serving plate. Spoon some risotto in and compress. Remove cutter and repeat with each serving. Cut chicken into 4–6 portions. (I used kitchen scissors.) Place a portion on each plate and serve.

masala chicken Serves 4

I love Indian food but find it very heavy sometimes. My take on this classic dish is a light way to enjoy all the spice and flavours of India. Remember when you are cooking Indian dishes, the flavours develop over time, so start preparations early to allow time for marinating meats.

INGREDIENTS

Boneless skinned chicken breasts	4
Lemon juice	3 Tbsp

MARINADE

Plain non-fat yoghurt	450 ml (15 fl oz / 1 3/4 cups)
Small onion	1, peeled and roughly chopped
Garlic	1 clove, peeled and crushed
Ginger	2.5-cm (1-in) knob, peeled and shredded with a grater
Red chilli powder	2 tsp
Garam masala	2 tsp

METHOD

- Start by preparing marinade. Put yoghurt, onion, garlic, ginger, chilli powder and garam masala in a blender and process until smooth. Set aside in a large bowl.

- Make about 4 cuts on each chicken breast to allow spices to be absorbed. Add chicken to marinade. If desired, cover and set the chicken aside in the refrigerator for up to a day for it to develop more flavour.

- When you are ready to cook, preheat the oven to 200°C (400°F). Place the chicken breasts slightly apart in a roasting pan and roast for 30–35 minutes until chicken is cooked through.

- Arrange chicken on serving plates with rice and vegetables of choice. Drizzle with lemon juice and serve.

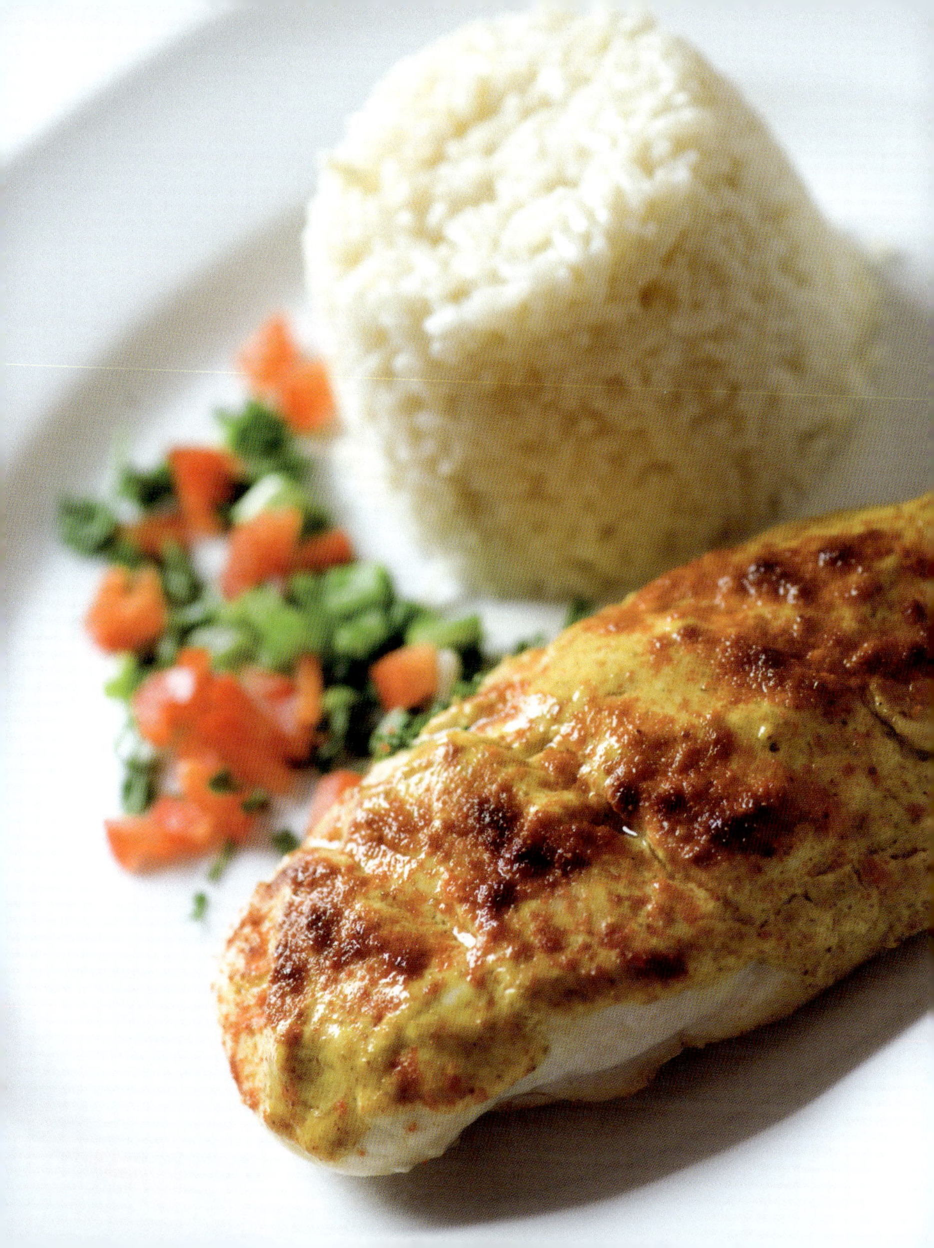

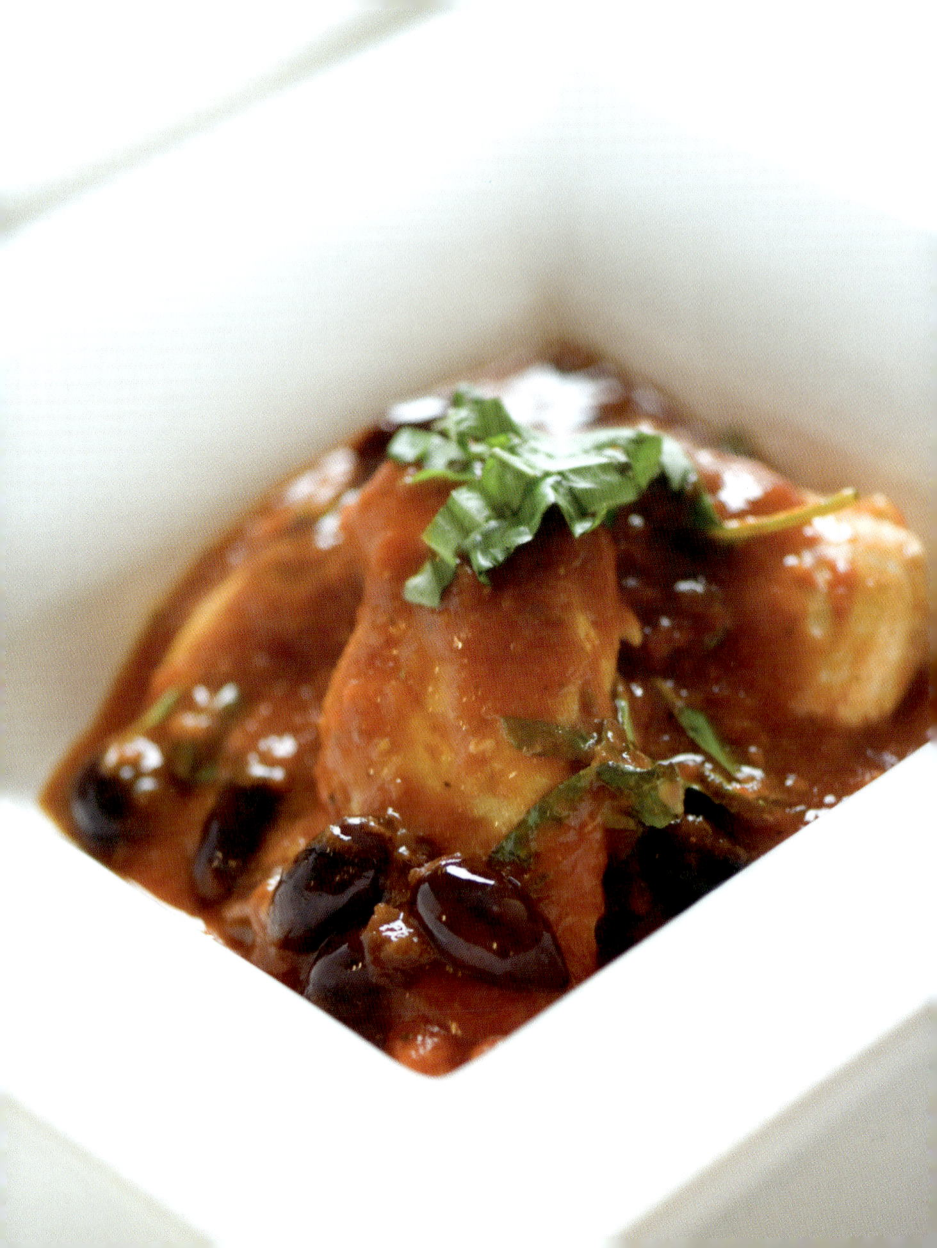

chicken napoli Serves 4

Italian cooking is so simple yet so delicious because they concentrate on using the best ingredients. Use the best ingredients you can find when preparing this dish. The chicken can be prepared with or without the skin on. As very little fat is used in this dish, it will still be rather healthy even with the chicken skin on.

INGREDIENTS

Olive oil	2 Tbsp
Chicken breasts	4
Canned chopped tomatoes	$1/2$ cup, processed in a blender
Sun-dried tomato paste	3 Tbsp (or process some sun-dried tomatoes in a blender with some olive oil)
Vegetable stock (page 9)	150 ml (5 fl oz)
Black olives (Greek olives are best)	12–16
Garlic	2 cloves, peeled and crushed

METHOD

- Heat olive oil in a large pan and sear chicken for a few minutes on each side.
- Add chopped tomatoes and tomato paste along with stock, olives and garlic. Lower heat and simmer for 30–40 minutes if there is bone on the breast, and 20–25 minutes if chicken is boneless. Let sauce thicken.
- Dish out and garnish as desired. Serve hot.

lemon chicken <small>Serves 4</small>

This Greek dish is always well received whenever I make it. It is so easy to prepare, as it is cooked in one dish and can be made up to a day in advance. If preparing ahead of time, just cover and keep the roasted chicken refrigerated and reheat in the oven before serving.

INGREDIENTS

Garlic	4 cloves, peeled and crushed
Honey	3 Tbsp
Olive oil	4 Tbsp
Lemons	6–8, halved
Chicken	1 whole, large, cut into 4–6 pieces
Garlic	4–6 cloves, left whole with skin on
Rosemary	1 sprig

METHOD

- Preheat the oven to 200°C (400°F).
- In a bowl, add crushed garlic, honey and olive oil. Squeeze the lemon juice into the bowl and set the lemons aside.
- Place the chicken in a roasting pan and pour over the marinade. Place the used lemon skins around chicken pieces. The lemon skins will add moisture to the chicken and release a delicious aroma when roasted. Add the whole garlic cloves and the rosemary.
- Roast in the oven for 1 hour or until the chicken is done.
- Serve the chicken with a salad.

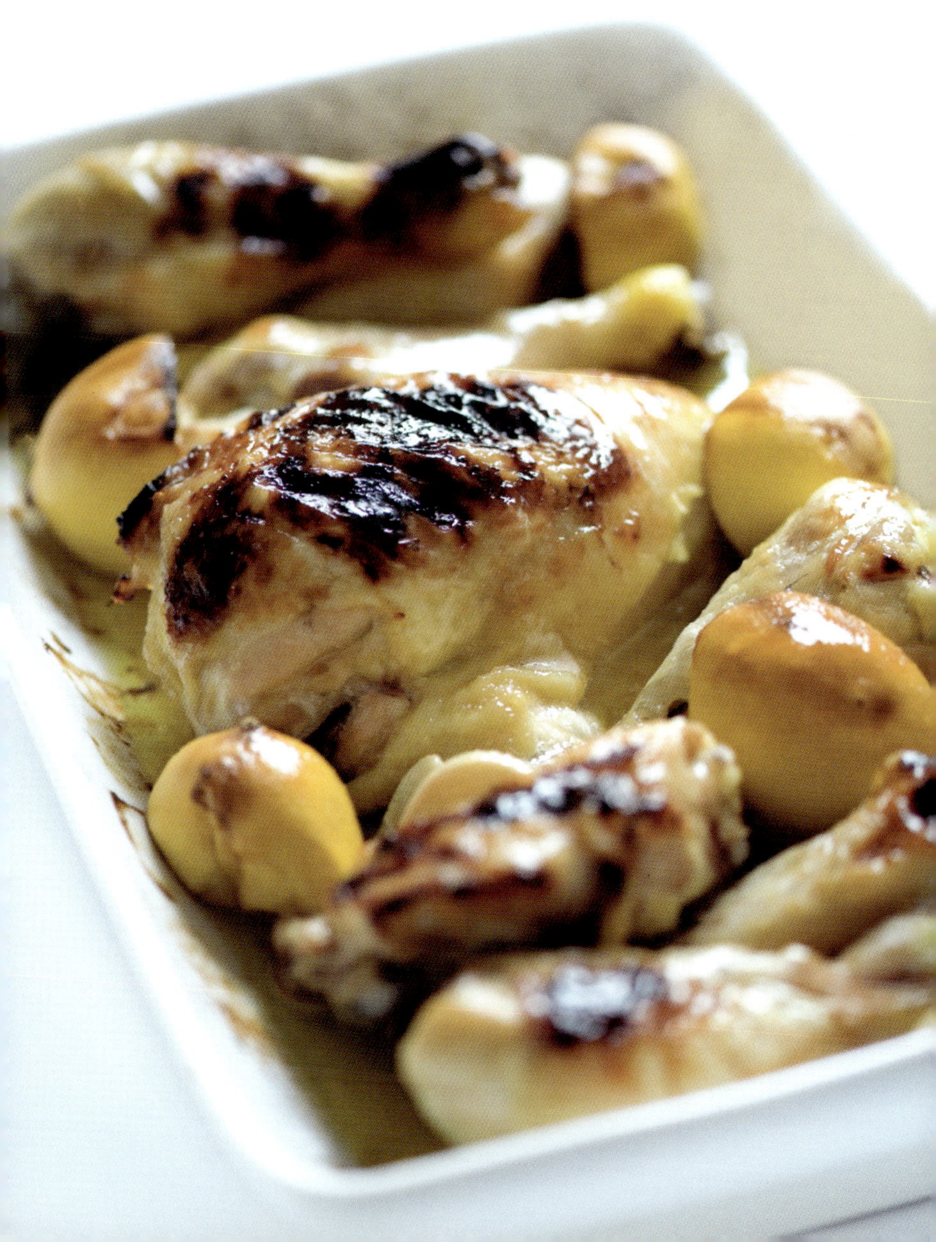

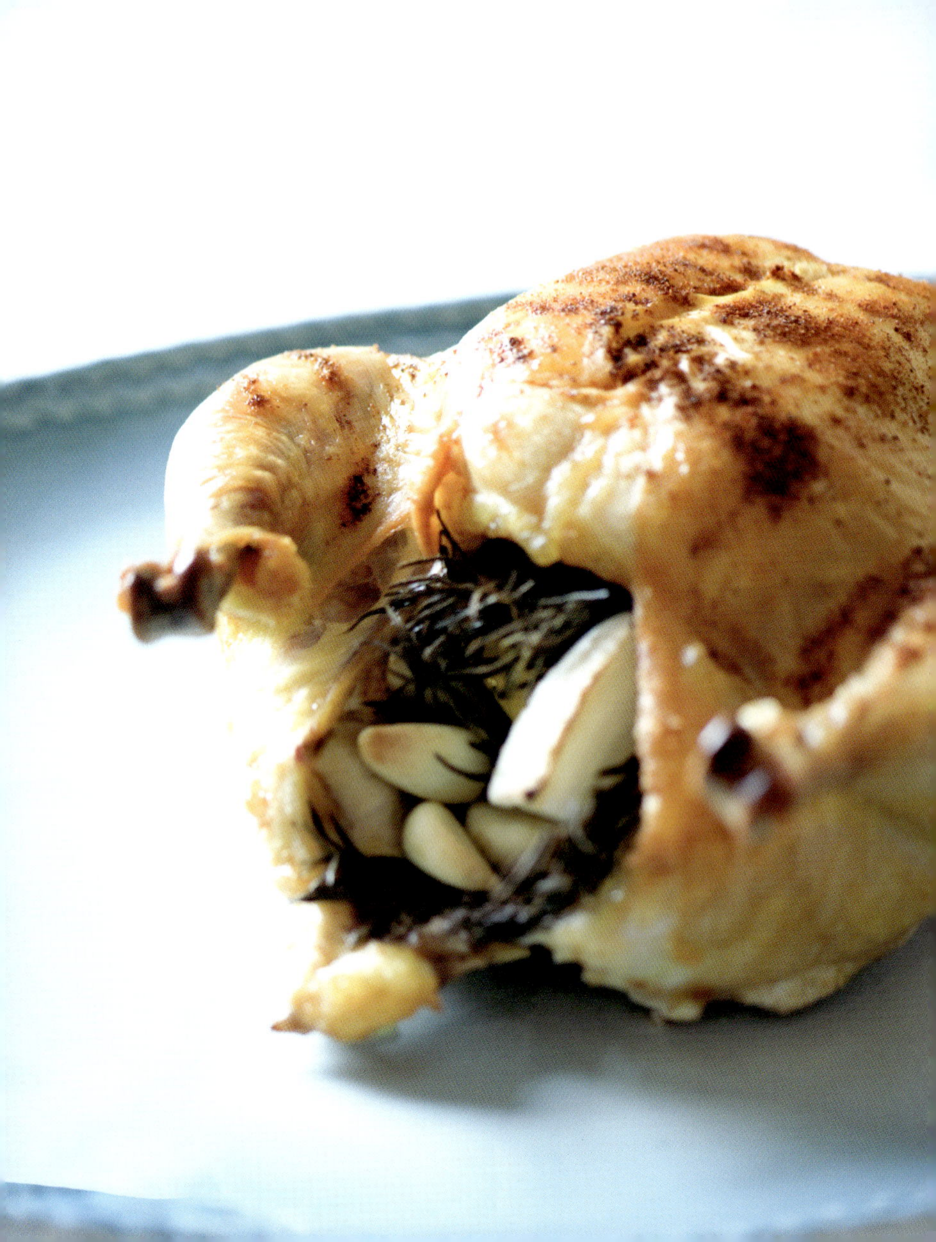

saffron chicken Serves 4

When I was filming a cooking show for the BBC in Dubai, I had the opportunity to go to the markets where saffron was available. Because it was so much cheaper than what I paid for it at home, I bought a lot of it and used it to make many dishes. This is one of my favourites. Remember, a little saffron goes a long, long way!

INGREDIENTS

Onion	1, peeled and cut into quarters
Garlic	4–6 cloves, peeled and cut into halves
Chicken stock cube	1, cut into quarters
Lemons	2; cut one into quarters
Large chicken	1, about 1.8 kg (3 lb)
Thyme	3 sprigs
Rosemary	3 sprigs
Saffron threads	1 tsp

METHOD

- Reheat the oven to 220°C (425°F).
- Clean the chicken and pat dry.
- Place the onion, garlic, stock cube and lemon quarters into the cavity of the chicken. This is typically done when roasting chicken in Spain and Italy.
- Lift up the skin of the chicken at the breast and push the thyme and rosemary under the skin. Place chicken breast side up in a roasting pan.
- Sprinkle the saffron on the chicken.
- Cut off the two ends of the remaining lemon and slice the lemon into 2.5-cm (1-in) thick slices. Place the lemon slices on top of the chicken and in between the legs. This will help keep the chicken moist and dissolve the saffron.
- Place the chicken in the oven for 1 hour, or until it is done.
- Serve the chicken with a salad.

roast lamb Serves 4

This Greek dish is simple but full of flavour. Ask your butcher for a lean cut of lamb when preparing this dish.

INGREDIENTS

Lamb steaks	4, each about 120 g (4 $^1/_2$ oz)
Salt	to taste
Freshly ground black pepper	to taste
Dried oregano	2 tsp
Potatoes	900 g (2 lb), peeled and sliced
Onions	2, peeled and sliced
Olive oil	3 Tbsp
Garlic	4 cloves
Water or chicken stock (page 9)	300 ml (10 fl oz / 1 $^1/_4$ cups)

METHOD

- Preheat the oven to 190°C (370°F).
- Sprinkle the steaks with salt, black pepper and 1 tsp oregano.
- Place potatoes and onions into a roasting pan and drizzle with olive oil. Sprinkle remaining oregano, salt and pepper over, then mix until the potatoes and onions are well coated with oil. Tuck the unpeeled garlic cloves among the potatoes. Place in the oven and roast until the potatoes are just starting to soften.
- Remove the roasting pan from the oven and place the lamb steaks on the potatoes. Pour over the water or chicken stock. Return the roasting pan to the oven and continue to roast for 30–35 minutes until the lamb is tender and the potatoes lightly brown at the edges.
- Serve the lamb with helpings of roasted potatoes.

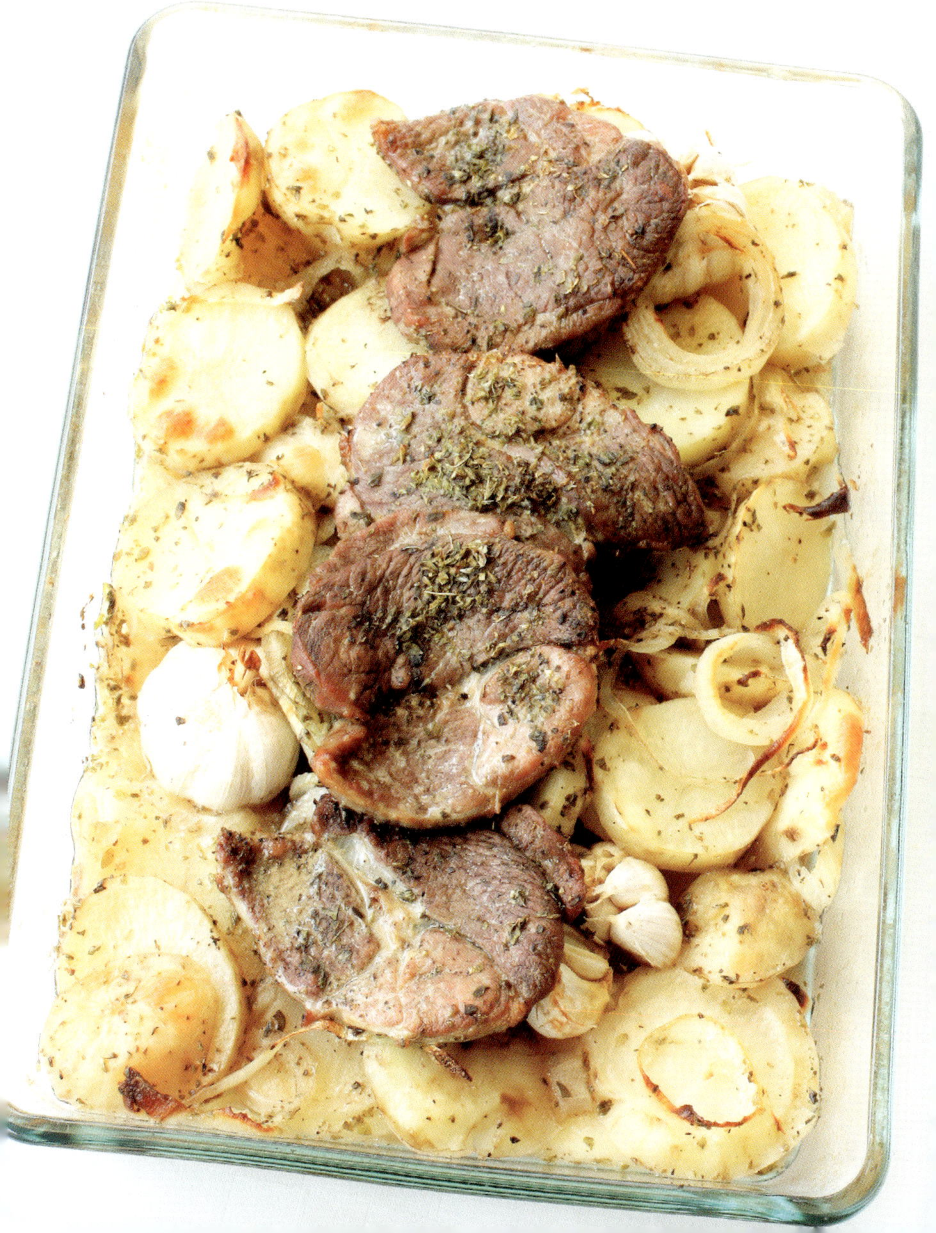

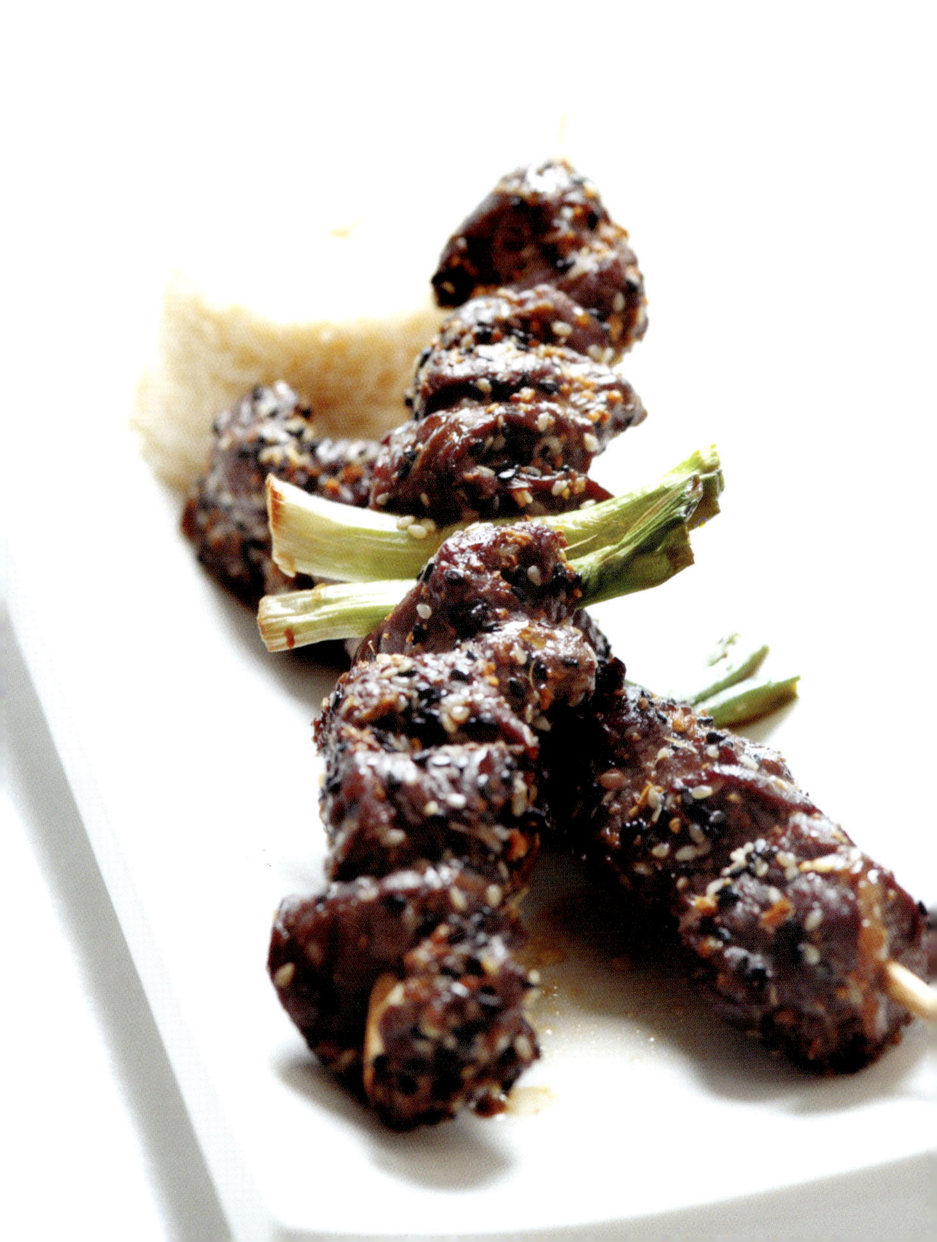

beef yakitori Serves 2–4

Yakitori is a great way to savour and enjoy meat. Recreate this experience in the comfort of your own kitchen!

INGREDIENTS

Beef	450 g (1 lb), fat trimmed and cut into cubes
Spring onions (scallions)	8, ends and leaves trimmed

TERIYAKI SAUCE

Japanese soy sauce (*shoyu*)	5 Tbsp
Sake	4 Tbsp
Mirin	1 Tbsp
Castor sugar	1 Tbsp

METHOD

- Combine all the ingredients for the teriyaki sauce in a pan over medium heat. Leave to simmer until thickened, then remove from heat and set aside to cool.

- When the sauce has cooled, place beef cubes in to marinade for at least 30 minutes.

- Divide beef cubes equally among 4 skewers if serving as a starter, or 2 if serving as a main course. Skewer the beef cubes with some spring onions.

- Grill for 5 minutes, turning skewers halfway through for even cooking.

- Serve immediately, with plain white rice if desired.

roasted vegetables Serves 6

I love roasted vegetables—it is such an easy-to-make dish and a winner all round. It is great as a side accompaniment to main dishes and filling enough to be a main dish. You can add some bacon or ham if you don't have to go vegetarian.

INGREDIENTS

Butternut squash	1, peeled and deseeded
Sweet potato	1, peeled
Carrots	3–4, peeled
Courgettes (zucchinis)	3–4
Button mushrooms	12
Brussels sprouts	12
Thick sliced white bread	4 slices, cut into 1-cm ($1/2$-in) cubes
Olive oil	4 Tbsp
Garlic	3 cloves, crushed
Fresh rosemary	3 sprigs
Fresh thyme	1 sprig
Salt	to taste
Ground black pepper	to taste

METHOD

- Preheat the oven to 220°C (440°F).

- Prepare the vegetables. Cut the butternut, sweet potato, carrots and courgette into 1-cm ($1/2$-in) cubes. Slice mushrooms and brussel sprouts into half.

- Place vegetables and bread cubes in a roasting pan. Add olive oil, garlic, herbs and salt and pepper. Toss well, making sure vegetables and bread cubes are well coated.

- Place in the oven to roast for 30–40 minutes, tossing vegetables occasionally.

- Serve hot.

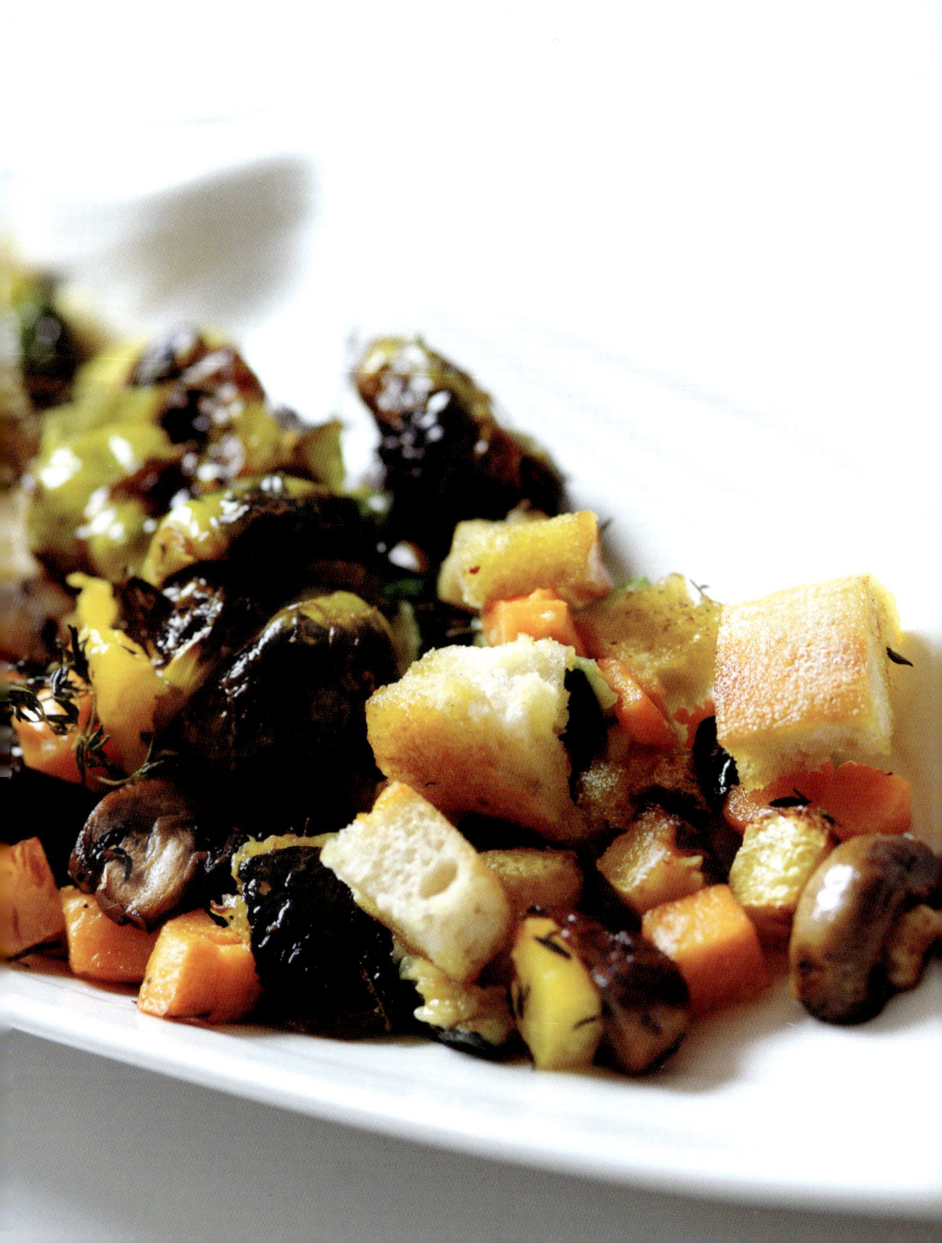

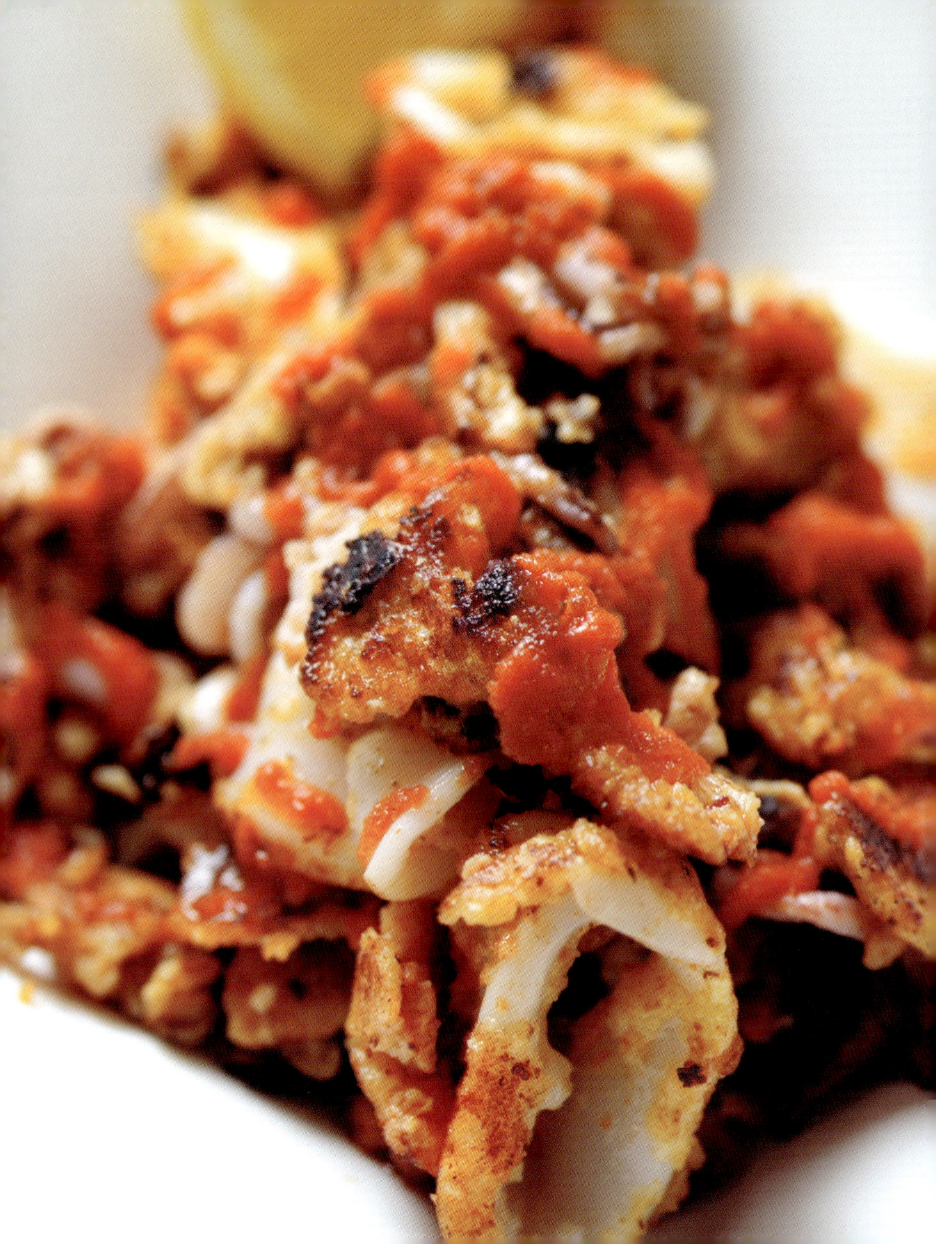

spicy chilli calamari serves 4

Coated in a simple batter of breadcrumbs, then lightly fried and dressed in a spicy, piquant sauce, this calamari dish certainly beats the usual deep-fried, battered versions served in most restaurants!

INGREDIENTS

Eggs	2
Day-old white bread	4–6 slices
Medium-size squid tubes	$1^1/_2$, cleaned and cut into even-size rings
Olive oil	2 Tbsp

SPICY TOMATO SAUCE

Olive oil	2 Tbsp
Tomato sauce	$1/_2$ cup
Sun-dried tomato paste	1 Tbsp (or process some sun-dried tomatoes in a blender with some olive oil)
Garlic	2 cloves, peeled and crushed
Red bird's eye chillies	3, chopped

METHOD

- Prepare spicy tomato sauce. Heat oil in a pan, then add remaining ingredients. Let mixture simmer over low heat for 3–4 minutes, then transfer to a blender and process until smooth. Set aside.

- In a bowl, beat eggs and set aside. Place bread in a blender and process into breadcrumbs. Place breadcrumbs on a plate and set aside.

- Heat oil in a large pan over high heat. Dip a handful of squid rings into beaten eggs, then coat with breadcrumbs. Fry squid rings for 3–5 minutes in small batches, so as not to overcrowd the pan and lower the cooking temperature. Remove and drain well.

- Toss calamari in spicy tomato sauce and serve immediately.

wasabi crust tuna Serves 4

Wasabi flavoured peas are served as snacks in some of the trendiest bars in Japan and around the world. I discovered it makes a fabulous crust on tuna, giving the tuna a great kick! Try it for yourself with this recipe.

INGREDIENTS

Wasabi-flavoured peas (from supermarkets)	1 cup
Sashimi-grade tuna	4 large steaks
Olive oil	2 Tbsp

METHOD

- Using a pestle and mortar, crush wasabi-flavoured peas almost to a powder. Alternatively, place peas in a plastic bag, seal and crush with a heavy rolling pin. Spread crushed peas out on a plate.
- Coat tuna steaks with crushed peas.
- Heat oil in a pan and sear tuna steaks for 2 minutes on each side.
- Serve hot with rice.

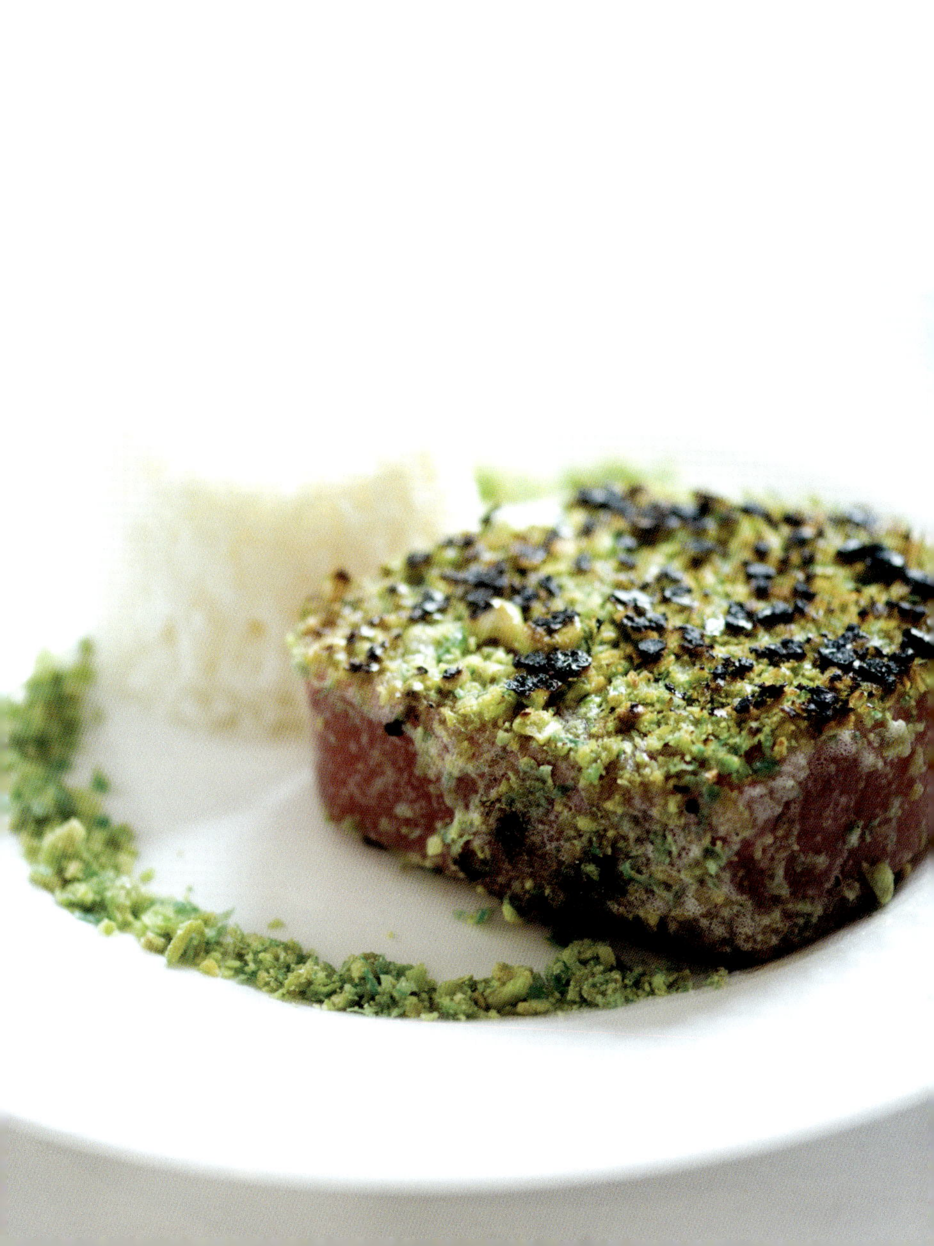

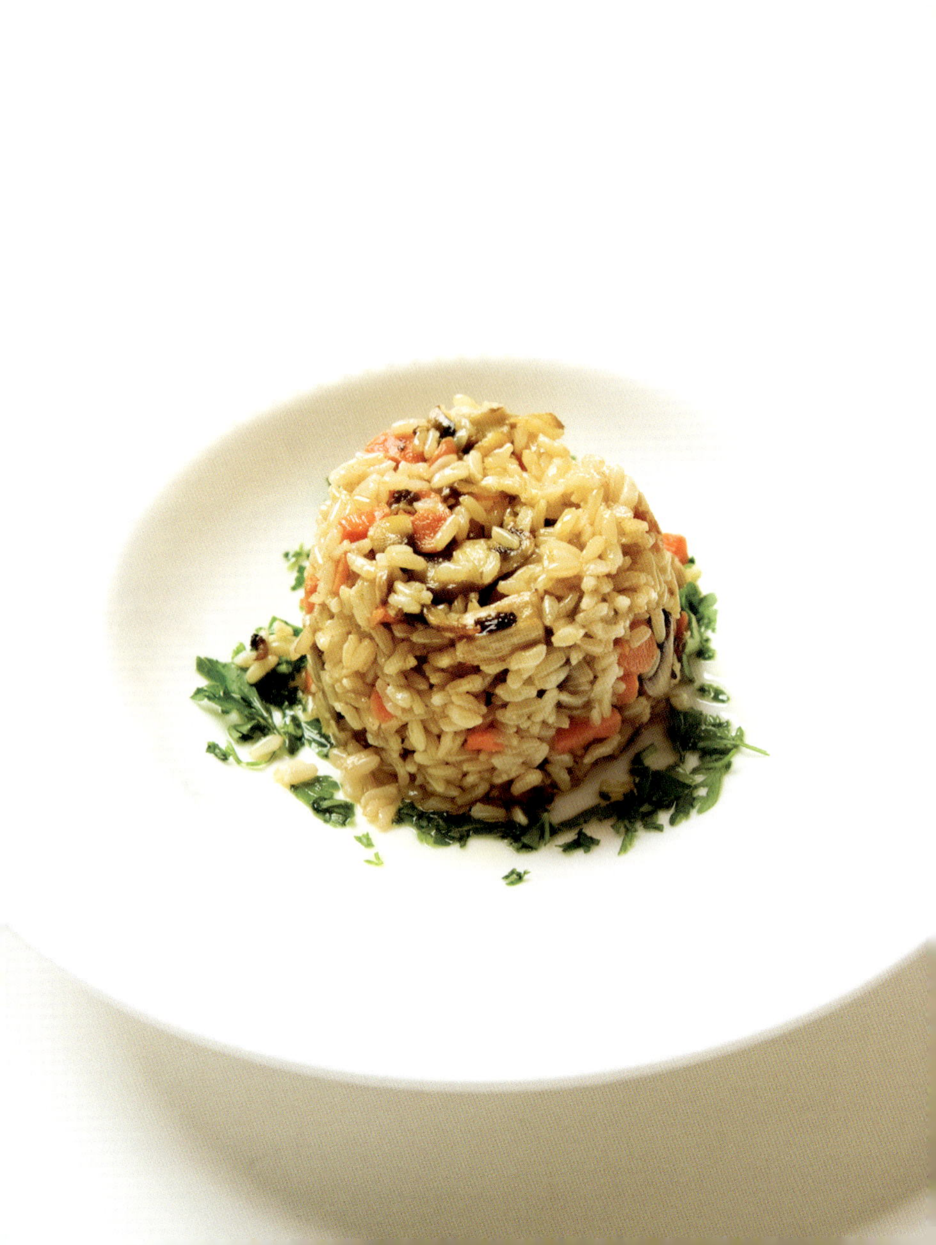

truffle risotto Serves 4

Truffles are terribly expensive, and rarely seen in domestic kitchens. However, you can recreate the flavour and aroma with truffle oil at less than half the cost!

INGREDIENTS

Truffle oil	6 Tbsp
Large onion	1, peeled and finely chopped
Large carrots	2, peeled and finely chopped
Garlic	2 cloves, peeled and crushed
Fresh shiitake mushrooms	6, caps wiped, thinly sliced
Button mushrooms	10–14, caps wiped, thinly sliced
Vegetable stock (page 9)	1 litre (32 fl oz / 4 cups)
Arborio rice	300 g (11 oz)
White wine (optional)	a few dashes
Fresh parsley (optional)	a handful, chopped

METHOD

- Heat 3 Tbsp of truffle oil in a pan over medium heat. Add onions and cook for 2–3 minutes, followed by carrots and garlic. Stir ingredients for a minute, then add mushrooms and cook for another minute. Meanwhile in a separate pot or pan, bring stock to the boil.

- Add arborio rice to pan with mushrooms and mix well. Add wine, if using, and leave to simmer for a minute. Add a ladle of stock at a time, stirring continuously for 20 minutes until creamy and tender. Add remaining truffle oil in the last minute of cooking.

- Garnish risotto with some fresh chopped parsley, if liked, and serve immediately.

egg fried rice Serves 4

Egg fried rice can be very greasy, but this is a light and flavourful version which I make for my little girl. She also loves it when I pack it for her lunch. It's a wonderful dish suitable for the whole family and so I'm dedicating this dish to Eleanor with love.

INGREDIENTS

Long-grain rice	450 g (1 lb)
Onion	1
Garlic	1 clove
Olive oil	as needed
Eggs	4, beaten
Sesame oil	2 Tbsp
Frozen peas	1½ cups
Oyster sauce	2 Tbsp
White sesame seeds	2 Tbsp
Light soy sauce	1 Tbsp
Spring onions (scallions)	6, chopped
Coriander leaves (cilantro)	a handful, chopped

METHOD

- Cook rice according to instructions on the pack a few hours or a day ahead. Fluff rice and set aside to cool. Refrigerate until needed.
- When ready to cook, peel and chop onion and garlic. Heat olive oil in a large pan and fry onion and garlic for a few minutes.
- Add eggs and scramble for 2 minutes. Add rice and other remaining ingredients. Mix well. Stir-fry until rice is heated through.
- Garnish with coriander leaves and serve.

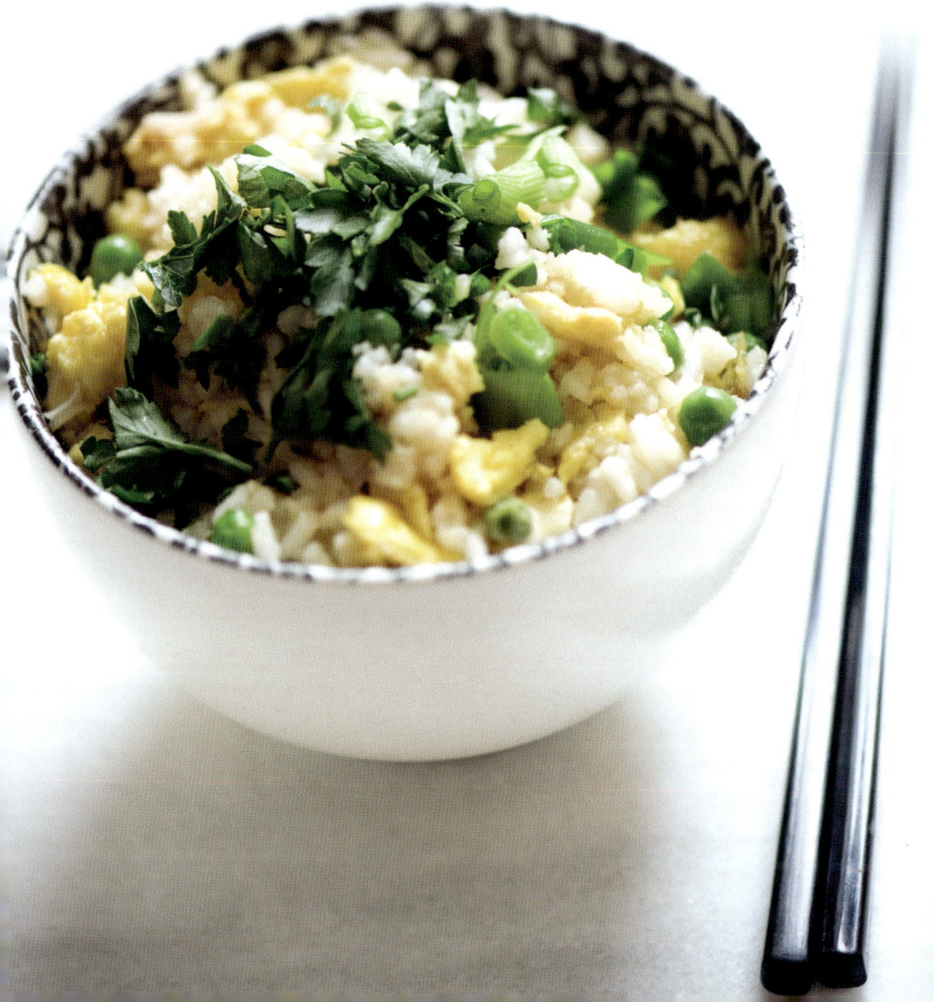

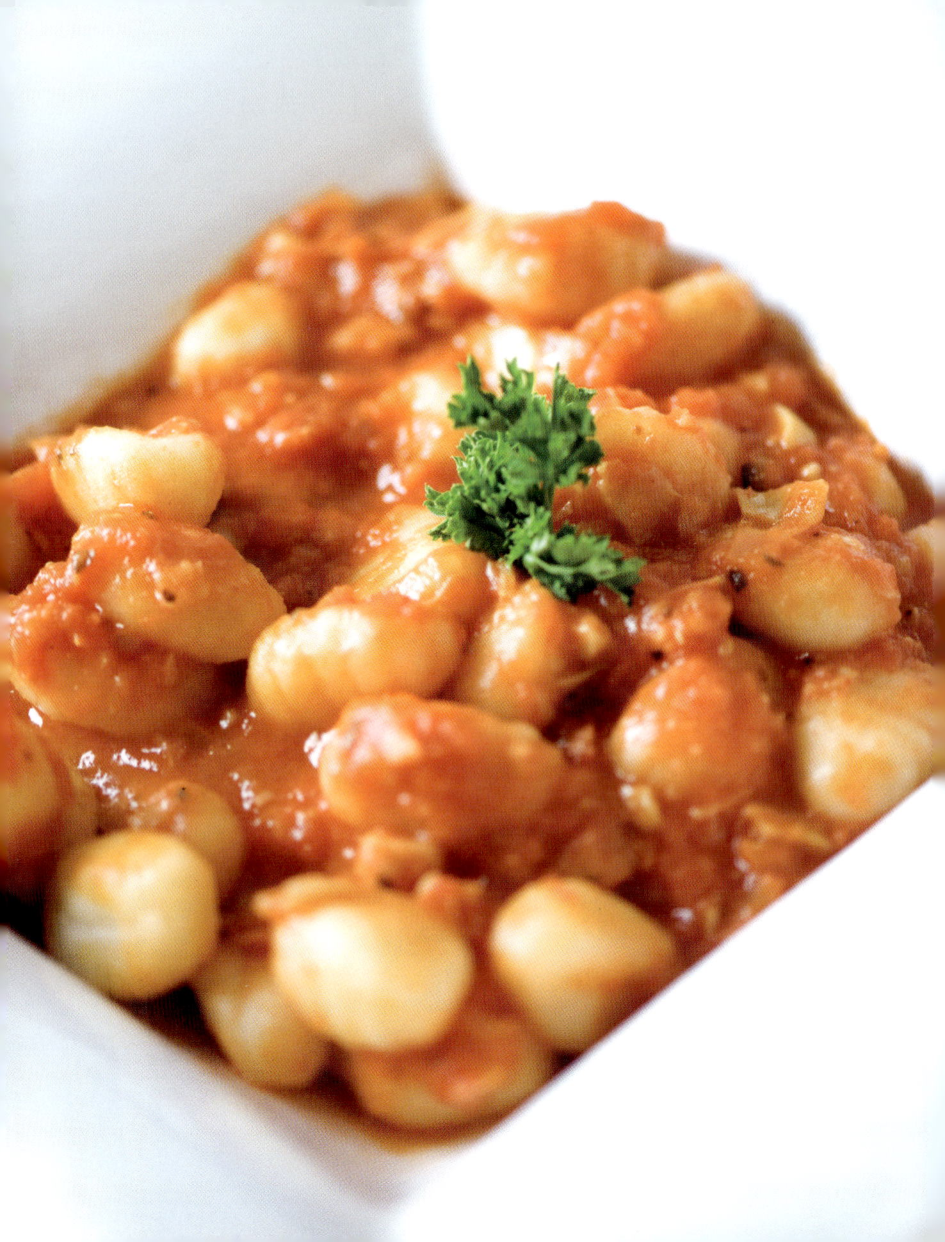

gnocchi in tomato sauce Serves 4

The form of gnocchi varies quite a lot throughout Italy. In the south, they are made large and very soft, and in the north, they are smaller and firmer, like what you would get in packets from the supermarkets outside of Italy.

INGREDIENTS

Fresh gnocchi	450 g (1 lb)
Garlic	1 clove, peeled and sliced
Tomato purée	250 ml (8 fl oz / 1 cup)
Sun-dried tomato paste	2 Tbsp (or process some sun-dried tomatoes in a blender with some olive oil)
Olive oil	2 Tbsp
Parsley	1 sprig

METHOD

- Bring a large pot of water to the boil. Add gnocchi. Gnocchi will sink to the bottom of the pan and float to the surface when they are ready. Takes 4–6 minutes. Drain and set aside.
- Heat olive oil in a large frying pan. Add garlic and cook for 30 seconds, then add tomato purée and paste. Cook over medium heat for about 3 minutes, then add gnocchi. Mix well for about a minute.
- Dish out and serve garnished with parsley.

tomato and crab spaghetti Serves 4–6

You really do not need the cheese and butter in a dish like this. This recipe is a perfect example of how you can enjoy a traditional Italian dish without having to travel to Italy!

INGREDIENTS

Spaghetti	450 g (1 lb)
Virgin olive oil	3 Tbsp
Garlic	1 clove, peeled and crushed
Cherry tomatoes	1 punnet, about 20, halved
Sun-dried tomato paste	2 Tbsp (or process some sun-dried tomatoes in a blender with some olive oil)
Sun-dried tomatoes	2 Tbsp, sliced
Fresh or canned crabmeat	1 cup (140 g / 5 oz)
Salt	to taste
Ground black pepper	to taste
Parsley	1 Tbsp, chopped

METHOD

- Bring a large pot of water to the boil. The trick to cooking pasta is to have as much water in as big a pot as possible. This prevents the pasta from sticking together when it gets starchy as it cooks. Once the water is at a rolling boil, add spaghetti and cook according to instructions on the pack.
- Heat oil in a large pan. Add garlic and turn heat down. Add cherry tomatoes and mix well.
- Add sun-dried tomato paste and sun-dried tomatoes, then remove from heat.
- Add crabmeat and season with salt and pepper. Add spaghetti and toss to coat well.
- Serve immediately with chopped parsley.

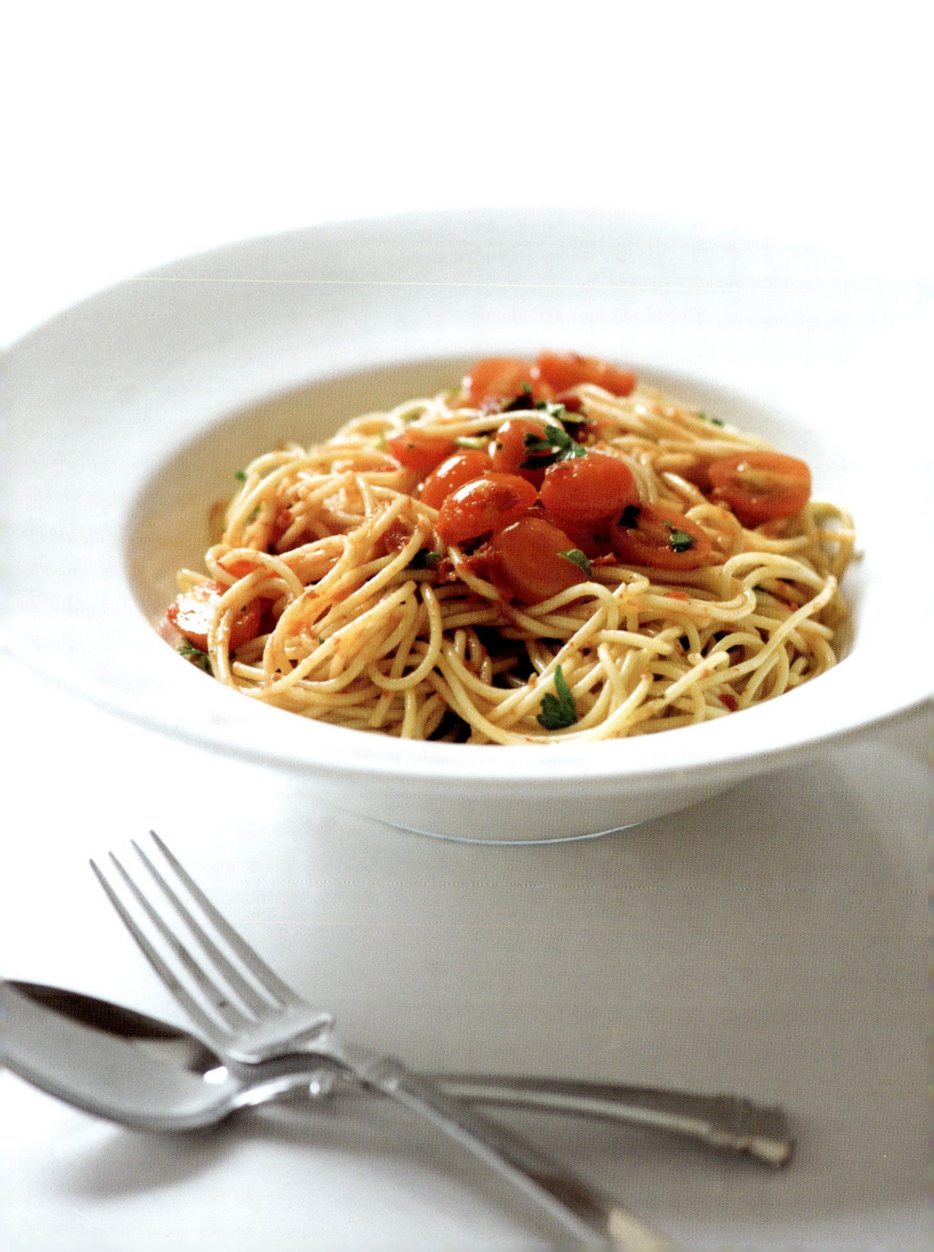

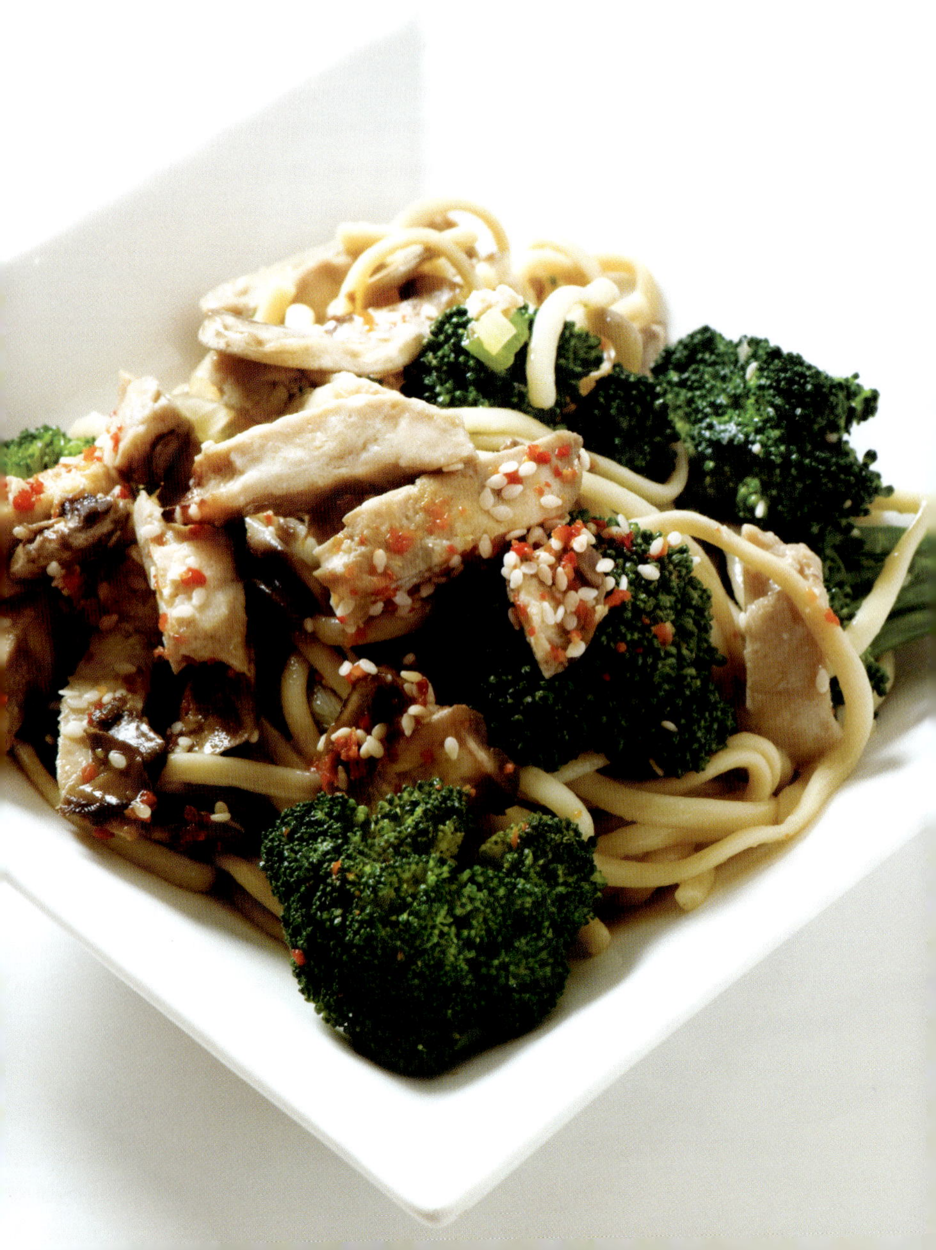

egg noodles with chicken and vegetables
Serves 4

This quick stir-fry is a popular Chinese restaurant favourite. However, the noodles are often very oily. This version uses minimal oil but yields fantastic results. Try it!

INGREDIENTS

Skinless chicken breasts	2, cut into strips
Mixed vegetables (broccoli, cauliflower, courgette (zucchini), mushrooms or carrots)	450 g (1 lb), cut into bite-size pieces
Water	125 ml (4 fl oz / $1/2$ cup)
Cooked egg noodles	300 g (11 oz)
Oyster sauce	1 Tbsp
Garlic	2 cloves, peeled and crushed
Red chilli	1, finely chopped
Toasted white sesame seeds (optional)	as desired

METHOD

- Heat about 1–2 Tbsp oil in a wok over medium-high heat. Add chicken strips and stir-fry for 3–5 minutes until chicken is cooked.

- Add mixed vegetables and stir to mix well. Add water and cook for 3–5 minutes until vegetables are tender.

- Add noodles, oyster sauce, garlic and chilli and toss ingredients to mix well. Allow mixture to simmer for another minute.

- Dish out. Garnish with sesame seeds if desired and serve immediately.

weights and measures

Quantities for this book are given in Metric, Imperial and American (spoon and cup) measures. Standard spoon and cup measurements used are: 1 tsp = 5 ml, 1 Tbsp = 15 ml, 1 cup = 250 ml. All measures are level unless otherwise stated.

Liquid And Volume Measures

Metric	Imperial	American
5 ml	1/6 fl oz	1 teaspoon
10 ml	1/3 fl oz	1 dessertspoon
15 ml	1/2 fl oz	1 tablespoon
60 ml	2 fl oz	1/4 cup (4 tablespoons)
85 ml	2 1/2 fl oz	1/3 cup
90 ml	3 fl oz	3/8 cup (6 tablespoons)
125 ml	4 fl oz	1/2 cup
180 ml	6 fl oz	3/4 cup
250 ml	8 fl oz	1 cup
300 ml	10 fl oz (1/2 pint)	1 1/4 cups
375 ml	12 fl oz	1 1/2 cups
435 ml	14 fl oz	1 3/4 cups
500 ml	16 fl oz	2 cups
625 ml	20 fl oz (1 pint)	2 1/2 cups
750 ml	24 fl oz (1 1/5 pints)	3 cups
1 litre	32 fl oz (1 3/5 pints)	4 cups
1.25 litres	40 fl oz (2 pints)	5 cups
1.5 litres	48 fl oz (2 2/5 pints)	6 cups
2.5 litres	80 fl oz (4 pints)	10 cups

Dry Measures

Metric	Imperial
30 grams	1 ounce
45 grams	1 1/2 ounces
55 grams	2 ounces
70 grams	2 1/2 ounces
85 grams	3 ounces
100 grams	3 1/2 ounces
110 grams	4 ounces
125 grams	4 1/2 ounces
140 grams	5 ounces
280 grams	10 ounces
450 grams	16 ounces (1 pound)
500 grams	1 pound, 1 1/2 ounces
700 grams	1 1/2 pounds
800 grams	1 3/4 pounds
1 kilogram	2 pounds, 3 ounces
1.5 kilograms	3 pounds, 4 1/2 ounces
2 kilograms	4 pounds, 6 ounces

Oven Temperature

	°C	°F	Gas Regulo
Very slow	120	250	1
Slow	150	300	2
Moderately slow	160	325	3
Moderate	180	350	4
Moderately hot	190/200	375/400	5/6
Hot	210/220	410/425	6/7
Very hot	230	450	8
Super hot	250/290	475/550	9/10

Length

Metric	Imperial
0.5 cm	1/4 inch
1 cm	1/2 inch
1.5 cm	3/4 inch
2.5 cm	1 inch

Abbreviation

tsp	teaspoon
Tbsp	tablespoon
g	gram
kg	kilogram
ml	millilitre